REAL
Abortion
Stories

The Hurting and The Healing

Edited by Barbara Horak

Strive For the Best Publishing
EL PASO, TEXAS

First printing 2007

ISBN-13: 978-0-9787551-3-3   ISBN-10: 0-9787551-3-8
LCCN: 2006906102

ATTENTION NONPROFIT ORGANIZATIONS, RELIGIOUS ORGANI-ZATIONS, AND OTHERS: Quantity discounts are available on bulk purchases of this book for educational, gift purposes, or as premiums for increasing magazine subscriptions or renewals. Special books or book excerpts can also be created to fit specific needs. For information, please contact Strive For the Best Publishing, 8900 Mettler Drive, El Paso, TX 79925-4047, (915) 591-2501; email Barbara@RealAbortionStories.com.

CONTENTS

PREFACE

These short, riveting stories by fourteen women and one man explain the desperate situations that drove each of them to choose abortion, describe their abortion experiences, tell of the heartbreaking aftermath of trauma and turmoil, and let us know how they found healing and peace. These first-person accounts reveal a side of the abortion issue that is seldom heard.

I appreciate the considerable effort by the contributors of these stories. Theirs was not an easy task, as they wrote their deeply personal stories. But in almost every case, these courageous storytellers said that the effort was therapeutic. And all hope that the telling of their experiences will help others steer clear of the mistakes they made, thereby avoiding the hurts they suffered.

For those who have already had an abortion, take heart. Others have experienced and overcome the same problems. These stories will demonstrate in a dramatic way that you are not alone and that healing from the traumatic aftermath of abortion is possible. The Appendix lists the organizations, programs and support groups, and resources that are available to help.

Some of the authors requested anonymity in order to protect the confidentiality of others; their names, presented in italics both in the Contents and at the end of their individual stories, are pseudonyms. The names of the persons mentioned within the stories have been changed to guard their privacy.

Chapter One

A Baby Would Interfere With My Education and My Life

I was something of a tomboy, playing every sport that I had time for: softball, basketball, track, and horseback riding. I was also on a clogging team. For those who don't know, clogging is sort of like tap dancing but the taps are loose and make a lot of noise. I had a great time competing with the team.

I have good parents and I had a good childhood. My mom and dad were married for twenty-five years before they divorced. We took vacations twice a year, a summer vacation and a winter skiing vacation. I had, what some would call, a privileged childhood.

Our family didn't go to church, and God wasn't talked about in our home. I don't remember hearing the name of Jesus until I was in high school. As a kid I tried to read the Bible, but I started at the beginning and got stuck in the chapter that says, so and so begat so and so, who begat so and so, and on and on.

I made good grades in high school and I didn't drink, smoke, or do drugs. I think the worst thing I did was break curfew and disrespect my parents. But I always had a boyfriend.

As a twenty-year-old college student, I met Mark. He was very possessive, and I finally broke up with him. Mark continued to pursue me. He wasn't abusive, he just wouldn't leave me alone. I moved 300 miles to another college to get away from him, but for several years I fearfully looked over my shoulder, afraid that he had found me.

In October, after we broke up, I was sick and thought I had the flu, so I went to the doctor. He told me I was pregnant. *Me? Pregnant! How could that be?* I was on the pill, and we had used condoms! When I told Mark, he wanted me to have the child. I didn't listen to him because I knew that a baby would keep him in my life forever.

I was almost three months along, and I was scared! I didn't think my parents would help me, and I didn't want to go on welfare. I still had a long way to go in school. I didn't know a thing about raising a child. I blamed God for allowing this to happen to me!

Some friends told me about a downtown abortion clinic. One of them had had an abortion, and she said she didn't regret a thing. I waited until the first day of Christmas break so my roommates would be gone, and I went to the clinic. I was four or five months pregnant, and I paid for the abortion with a credit card I had recently received.

When I woke up in the recovery room, I looked at the nurse standing next to me. I remember asking her, "Is it okay if I cry now?" She said, "Okay." I started crying. She walked away.

I realized what I had done—I had just destroyed the life of my child. Looking back, I am so thankful I was put to sleep, so I have no recollection of the actual abortion procedure.

Our apartment was a three-story townhouse. The living room and the kitchen were on the second floor and my bedroom was on the third floor. I felt so bad I could not climb the stairs to my bedroom, so I laid on the couch in the living room. For a week, I crawled to the kitchen and bathroom. I bled so much, I hoped I was dying. Finally, I felt well enough to crawl up to my bedroom. I took a shower, plastered a smile on my face, and went home for Christmas.

After that, life was a blur. I moved like a zombie, although I went to class; I went to work; I went out with my friends. I had two one-night stands and I got pregnant again. I didn't know who the father was. I had my second abortion three months after the first one.

Zombie mode took over again. I attempted to mask the pain with alcohol. I didn't care about school. Or work. Or friends. Or family. I didn't care about anything. I was a walking, talking heartache. At times the dark, heavy pain was so overwhelming, I had trouble breathing. It was as though I was trying to move through quicksand, but was being sucked down. I felt used. Abandoned. Ugly. Unwanted. Unloved.

I wanted the pain to end. I didn't care if I died. Even though a serial rapist was stalking women near campus, I would walk around alone after midnight. I don't know why. I just didn't care, and I wanted the pain to end.

Two months later I met Brian. He became my newest boyfriend. He was the closest thing to an angel I'd ever met. He had grown up in church and told me he wouldn't marry anyone who didn't go to church. So I gritted my teeth and attended church with him.

Soon after I started dating Brian, the nightmares began. Every night I dreamed that Mark was stalking me. He killed Brian and grabbed me. He was doing this because I had aborted his baby. I would scream the whole time he was hurting Brian. I pleaded with Mark to stop, that Brian had nothing to do with the death of our child. This recurring nightmare lasted six months. I hated to go to bed and I got very little rest during that time.

During this time Brian told me about a man, named Jesus. I told him about a girl, named Heather. Me. The more I told him about me, the more he told me about Jesus.

The girl who was unlovable...Jesus loved her!

The girl who was dying inside…Jesus wanted to make her alive!

The girl who had done the most detestable thing a human can do…Jesus wanted to forgive her and forget that it ever happened!

The girl whose heart was broken beyond recognition…Jesus wanted to put it back together and make it brand-new!

Brian gave me a Bible for my birthday in September. For the first time since I was a child, I read it. This time I read from the New Testament.

We dated for six months. It's a wonder he stuck with me that long. I was an emotional basket case: either extremely depressed or extremely happy. And very clingy. I had always required a lot of time and energy from anyone I dated, but the depression caused by my abortions magnified this neediness to a whole new level. I literally smothered Brian with my demands for his attention.

After we broke up, I still went to church. I couldn't get enough of this Jesus person, and I had a lot of questions that needed to be answered. One night after a Wednesday college group meeting, I went to the library to study. I couldn't seem to focus on the textbook I was reading. I read the same page over and over, but I just couldn't grasp the contents. I sat there staring at the page, wondering what was going on.

Then I heard it. I heard it clearly. A voice whispered to my heart and said, "It's time, Heather. It's time." I understood exactly what that meant and I didn't hesitate. The best way I knew how, I prayed.

I said, "God, I'm a horrible, wretched person who has done unthinkable things. Can You and will You forgive me? I know that You told Jesus to die for me. I'll never understand that, but I believe it. I hate my life, please change it. I hate myself, please change me. I need You and all that You are. Please live in me. Amen."

That night when I fell asleep, I had a dream. It was not the recurring nightmare; in this dream I was standing alone in what appeared to be a field of smoke, the kind that doesn't choke you but swirls around. Or maybe it was clouds. But everything was white.

Movement caught my eye and I looked to see what it was. It was a man dressed in white walking toward me. He had long straight white hair and a white beard. As he got closer, I didn't feel alarmed or afraid. I noticed that he was carrying a bundle in his arms. When he was really close, I looked at his eyes: They were filled with love. His face radiated calm and peace and love.

When he stopped, he was just an arm's length away. I looked closer at the bundle he was carrying. Then I realized, the bundle was a baby. *How cute*, I thought. The man tilted the baby toward me a little, and I looked closer. It hit me. This was my baby! I was looking at the most beautiful child I have ever seen!

I couldn't breathe. I wanted to ask, "Why have you done this? Why did you bring my baby out here? Are you trying to torture me for the wrong I've done?"

I looked again at his face. He didn't look like he was enjoying this moment of my incredible pain. Then, just like in the library, he spoke directly to my heart. He said, "My Heather, since you have accepted My Child into your heart and life, you will get to see your children when you get to heaven." After He said that, He walked away, with tears in His eyes.

I woke up from the first good night's rest I had had in years, with a feeling of peace like I had never known. I remember that dream as though it happened last night, and I have never had another dream like that. My nightmares about Mark stalking me and killing Brian stopped that same night.

Even though I knew very little about the Bible, I somehow always knew that my babies were in heaven and that God watched over them. Now I know when I get to heaven, after I see my Lord God and my Lord Jesus, I get to see my babies!

That October, less than a year after my two abortions, the old Heather started fading away, and the new Heather started taking shape. I had finally found peace. I didn't need a guy to "complete" me. I quit smoking and drinking, cold turkey, and never had any withdrawal symptoms. I quit cursing and sleeping around. I began really studying my Bible and went to everything the church offered. I smiled and laughed.

Even though I walk through the valley of the shadow of death.... (Psalm 23:4a)

I had walked through that valley feeling all alone, as though the world was out to get me. But I didn't just survive, thanks to God; I came out more alive than I have ever been! I have learned that when you give up the old self, God replaces it with something new and much better!

For three years after my abortions, I avoided being around small children. Then one day I was standing in the hallway of our church when a young mother needed to run and do something quickly. She thrust her baby into my arms and hurried off. I started crying.

A friend, standing nearby, said, "Do you want me to take the baby?"

"No," I said, "I have to face the pain and reality someday. Why not now when I'm surrounded by people who love me?"

♦   ♦   ♦

It has been nine years since I met Jesus and invited Him into my heart, to be the Lord of my life. Not once, not ever, have I regretted that decision! I only regret that I didn't meet Him earlier in my life.

I can testify to the truth of the words in the song, *He Lives*.

> You ask me how I know He lives?
> He lives within my heart.

◆ ◆ ◆

What has happened since meeting Jesus is better than anything I could have imagined for myself! I am now married to an amazing man of God! Stephen isn't perfect, but he's perfect for me. He is generous, kind, gentle, funny, loving, and patient. He's the man I dreamed of for so many years, and the man I had prayed for after I met Jesus. He was a virgin when we got married, and he is wonderfully forgiving of my past. We have been married for three years, and it has been the most wonderful challenge and adventure I have ever had! I am blown away by this man that God allowed me to marry, and I have grown closer to Jesus because of Stephen.

And get this. We only dated for two weeks before we became engaged, and we were married five months later. Because I knew he was the one that God had prepared just for me, I married a virtual stranger! I respect, adore, love, and cherish him! And I thank God for him daily!

When I didn't get pregnant, I worried that this might be because of possible injuries caused by my abortions. I finally found a doctor who took my concerns seriously and he did some tests. I am so grateful that God spared me. I have no scar tissue, no problem in my uterus, and nothing wrong with my tubes or my ovaries. I think there is only one reason why we have not gotten pregnant—it's not God's time. I believe my womb will be closed and empty until He opens it and fills it with children.

If this does not happen, I believe He will turn our hearts toward adoption.

◆   ◆   ◆

I weep for joy every time I hear the words of that beautiful hymn, *Amazing Grace*, because it so perfectly describes my life.

> Amazing grace! how sweet the sound,
> That saved a wretch like me!
> I once was lost, but now am found,
> Was blind, but now I see.
> 'Twas grace that taught my heart to fear,
> And grace my fears relieved;
> How precious did that grace appear
> The hour I first believed.
>
> —Heather Thrower Gibbs

Chapter Two

My Boyfriend Said, "It's Up To You"

I was raised in the Catholic Church and went to Catholic schools through the eleventh grade. As a high school senior, I was into dancing, drinking, and boys. In October of that year, I had to tell my parents that I was pregnant and planned to get married in December. I never considered abortion.

So, at seventeen, I became a bride and in the spring I had my first child, a boy. My second child, another boy, was born twenty-two months later. Because I was so young when I got married, I missed out on a lot. As I thought about these things, I resented that I had missed the senior prom, high school graduation, and the opportunity to attend college. When I was thirty, I had a baby girl.

My husband was the domineering type, and I felt like I couldn't do anything without his permission. I longed for my freedom. I thought I could make it without him, and began thinking about leaving him. After fourteen years of marriage, I finally made the decision to leave. I felt inferior and was intimidated by my husband, so I gave in to his demands for custody of our boys, who were twelve and fourteen, and I took the baby who was eighteen months old.

At the age of thirty-three, I met Jim. Jim was also divorced and had a child by his first wife. He also had a daughter from another relationship. We dated for a while, and I got pregnant. I asked for his opinion about our pregnancy and he said, "It's up to you; do what you want to do." Because neither he nor I wanted more children, and because I had already felt like a failure as a parent, I made the decision to abort our child.

I was determined that no one would ever find out about the abortion. I married Jim but we never talked about it. Only he and I and the people at the abortion clinic would ever know. I put the abortion experience out of my mind.

A year later, I was pregnant again. Jim left the decision up to me. I had my second abortion. When I got home, I collapsed in my husband's arms, sobbing, "I can't believe I did it again." I took all the blame because my husband would have done anything I wanted him to.

This time, I dug a deep hole, and I buried the pieces of my heart that died with my babies, and began building a sturdy wall around that secret place, so I would never hurt like that again.

Eventually I accepted Jesus Christ as my Savior and confessed my sins, even the hidden sins of my abortions. And although He forgave me, I did not forgive myself and did not deal properly with my painful secrets of abortion. It was not until seven years later at a Beth Moore Conference that I let God begin to heal those broken parts of my heart.

Soon afterward, I was listening to a radio program from Focus on the Family and heard two women talking about the symptoms of Post-Abortion Syndrome. I was amazed; I had suffered from almost every one of the traumatic symptoms that they listed. These women had written a book, *Her Choice to Heal*. I immediately ordered a copy. Even after I read the book and did the journaling, I felt I needed something more. I still hadn't told anyone about my abortions. I remembered the women in the radio interview talking about post-abortion counseling, so I looked in the phone book for a crisis pregnancy center. I called the Pregnancy Decision Health Center to ask about counseling, and they said they had a HEART (Healing the Effects of

Abortion-Related Trauma) group starting the very next week. I felt this was God-sent. I was interviewed and started with the group the following Monday. God is so good!

This HEART group was led by post-abortive women. For the first time I was finally able to tell my story in a safe place where I wasn't judged. This loving group allowed me to grieve for my children. Our society says this is not necessary, but I know differently. I named my babies and gave them to Jesus. It was as though I had allowed the light of God's love to shine into my deep hurtful hole of hidden secrets.

Although this healing process was difficult and heartrending, it was so freeing. God's healing grace changed my life! I felt my life was stagnant, until I finally left my heavy burden of regret and guilt and anger and shame at the foot of the cross. Through this involvement with HEART, God was able to guide me on my healing journey.

When the HEART group was over, I still felt I needed to do more, so I took training to become a group leader for the HEART program. In the midst of that training, I gave my testimony at a women's weekend retreat for my church. Twenty-one women heard my story, and later six of them came to me and secretly told me they were post-abortive and how important my testimony had been to them. What a blessed God-orchestrated experience. This confirmed my mission and my resolve to tell others about the healing grace of Jesus. Statistics indicate that one in every four women is post-abortive; the ratio of the post-abortive women at the retreat supports that statistic. Now I look around at the women in my church and wonder, "Who else is suffering in silence?"

I had the opportunity to join a group of women who were gathering on the steps of the State Capitol on the 30th anniversary of *Roe v. Wade.* Each held a sign that read "I Regret My Abortion." I was invited to be one of fifteen women who would give their testimonies. I knew the event would be widely covered by the media.

My two daughters did not know about my abortions, and I was afraid they or someone they knew would see me on television. So the day before the Capitol event, I sat down with each one of them and asked, "Do you know what happened on January 22, thirty years ago?" Neither of them had a clue, so I told them about the Supreme Court decision of *Roe v. Wade* that was decided on that day. Then I told them about my abortion experiences. Immediately I felt such a sense of relief; I no longer had to hide this secret from them or worry about them finding out.

These wonderful daughters have been very supportive of my efforts to help other post-abortive women find the healing they so desperately need, in Christ. My youngest daughter is a psychology major and after hearing my story, she did her internship at a Pregnancy Distress Center.

A story can change a life! A story can also save a life! I tell my story in the hopes it will save innocent babies and prevent pain and suffering to their mothers and dads.

◆   ◆   ◆

The author of this story, Cathie, had the opportunity to speak in her church recently. After hearing her testimony, her friend, Krista, wrote the following:

> *I am so proud of Cathie for stepping out of her comfort zone and speaking the truth. If I close my eyes, I can see the confrontation between Satan and the demons on that Sunday afternoon after Cathie's testimony. Not all was well in the fiery pit....*
> **Satan** *(gritting his fangs): "Who was in charge of Cathie Hilton?"*
> **Fear** *(trembling in his boots): "That would be me, your royal ugliness."*
> **Satan**: *"How could this happen?"*
> **Fear**: *"I don't know, sir, I mean, I thought that I had her. I had shackles on her feet. I had her tongue tied up. I had it*

glued to the roof of her mouth. I had my talons deep in her brain as recently as two weeks ago! I can't believe that this happened!"

Satan: *"Get away from me, you sniveling wretch. Doubt, where are you?"*

Doubt: *"Here, father of darkness."*

Satan: *"You said that she would never get out of your snare. What happened?"*

Doubt: *"Well, sir, I am not sure. One minute she was in utter darkness and the next thing I knew, she was learning scripture and praying and looking for help. She found an accountability partner and people to encourage her. The next thing I knew, she was punching holes in the darkness with God's Word. Even so, I never saw this coming! I thought that she was useless to the Kingdom of God."*

Satan: *"Whatever. Send me Despair."*

Despair: *"Woe is me. What are we going to do? She has put the word out that there is healing to be had for the asking. Life will never be the same in their lives again. Gloom, despair, and agony on me. Deep dark depression, excessive misery…"*

Satan: *"Enough. You are killing me here. Bitterness, front and center."*

Bitterness: *"She was mine, prince. I had her heart so hardened that she should never have gotten to this place of redemption. She told her friend that she was going to read from a paper about the healing group and that would have to be enough, then her other friend laid hands on her and prayed and then—"*

Satan: *"You blithering idiots. She has escaped captivity. She has taken others with her. More will follow, you know, as the Word gets out. Jesus won one more round today. Before long, He will have won them all. One by one, He wins hearts, you know. If we don't keep our captives blinded* *to His Truth, we will lose. Now get out there and take hostages!"*

Fear: *"Sir, do you want us to go back to Cathie?"*

Satan: *"NO! She is lost to us! She believes. She walks her talk and talks her walk. Move on!"*

◆ ◆ ◆

Jesus: *"Yes, she is Mine. She can do all things through Me. They are all mine. One by one, they will come home to me again, and I will run to them and dry their tears. I am the Victor. One day, Satan, you will kneel to me as well. Until that day, your powers of evil may win the skirmish, but they will not win the war. I have come that all may have Life and have it more abundantly. My Word illuminates and sets the captives free!"*

Cathie:

"Greater is He who is in me than he who is in the world.
  God is who He says He is
  God can do what He says He can do
  I am who God says I am
  I can do all things through Christ
  God's Word is alive and active in me
  And I'm believin' God!"

—Cathie Hilton

Editor's note: The HEART group that helped Cathie is a program of Heartbeat International. To locate a group near you, contact the Option Line at 1-800-395-HELP (395-4357).

The book that helped Cathie is *Her Choice to Heal: Finding Spiritual and Emotional Peace After Abortion,* by Sydna Massé and Joan Phillips. It is available at www.RamahInternational.org. or http://GriefNet.org.

Focus on the Family can be contacted at 1-800-A-Family (232-6459) or at www.family.org.

Chapter Three

I Paid for My Mistress' Abortion—For Many Years!

It was March 1984. The bile rose in my throat, and the flight reflex in my body had me ready to jump and run! But Susan was so calm, it was eerie; I thought, *If she can take it, I can.*

How could I have let this happen? Wasn't I happily married to my second wife, "master of my own destiny," "captain of the ship," owner of two successful businesses, respected in the community? Yet here I was, cowering in a Planned Parenthood office looking for a referral for an abortion. An abortion that would not only end a pregnancy, but that would allow me to cover up this yearlong, illicit love affair that had gotten so far out of hand.

My normally clear thinking had been totally thrown off track by this pretty twenty-one-year-old. First had been the innocent office flirtations, then the pride in having someone like her interested in me, then the doubts about my second marriage, then a weekend trip to Mexico together. I was hooked…in love, in lust, and involved way too far. If only this "problem" would go away, perhaps I could escape this affair and save the horrific loss that usually comes to businessmen who leave their wives for a young secretary.

The counselor came in and said the pregnancy test was indeed positive and asked what we wanted to do about this "situation."

Without hesitation, Susan said, "I want to terminate the pregnancy. I'm not ready to raise a child by myself." Then she nodded her head toward me, and said, "He won't be able to help."

I winced. It occurred to me that we had never discussed the possibility of us ending up together. The counselor never spoke directly to me during the thirty-minute session. She and Susan discussed the abortion as though I wasn't even present. Apparently this decision was Susan's to make. I was just expected to foot the bills and "be there" for her. We were given an appointment for the next Thursday at Reproductive Services in El Paso.

The next five days were agony for me. I had been raised to believe that babies were gifts from God. In fact, just out of high school when my girlfriend became pregnant, we were married and my son, Dale, was born. Sylvia was born three years later. Of course, I remember the sleepless nights and the fears of young parenthood, but these children were and still are the joy of my life. And yet here I was ready to sacrifice a child for the sake of convenience and finances. I drank heavily every night seeking relief from my confusion.

I covered my absence with another business trip, and Susan and I drove to El Paso the night before the "procedure." That evening in the hotel room, I threw out the options of adoption, of Susan moving out of town, and of me leaving my wife. None of these was acceptable to Susan. The simpler option seemed to be to just eliminate the problem. Sitting on the bed, I began to cry. I knew this wasn't right.

To quiet me, Susan sat next to me and told me why she was able to remain so calm. "I've already had an abortion," she said. She described it as "no big deal." If she had gone through this experience before and was okay with it again, I decided to hold onto that. It would be "no big deal" for me either.

But Susan had failed to tell me the "rest of the story." It would be years later before I realized how difficult Susan's life had already been. And I had no idea how our decision to end this pregnancy would complicate my own life!

The next morning we kept the eight o'clock appointment at the downtown abortion clinic. We registered as though it was a regular doctor's office; the receptionist behind a glass window thrust a sign-in sheet toward us. I was seated in a waiting room as Susan was ushered into a back office. I was told that she would be fine, and we could go home in an hour or two.

There was no conversation in the waiting room I shared with five women and two men. It appeared the others, like me, were waiting to take a friend home after the "procedure." I glanced at the outdated magazines scattered on the table next to my chair. On three occasions new clients walked in, but there was no eye contact. Everyone stared at the floor. Knowing what was occurring in the next room made the wait seem long. Four women came out and left with their companions. About an hour later a nurse motioned me aside and told me that Susan was fine, but she needed to rest for a while.

When she was ready to leave, I took her to a Chinese restaurant. As we ate, I asked her if she was okay. The third time I asked, she snapped, "I'll be fine; just don't ask me again!" We finished the meal in silence.

Back at the hotel we napped for three hours, watched some television, and then went to a movie. That night Susan cried because of the extreme cramps. In the shower, I cried out loud, feeling ashamed for feeling relieved.

I thought it was over. I was wrong.

◆ ◆ ◆

Fast forward three years and you will find me divorced from wife number two, living with, and then marrying Susan. I was living out every sick sexual fantasy imaginable. You see, Susan was bisexual, and often shared her female lovers with me. She even had me pick up one-night stands for "us," and we joined a swingers' club.

These sexual orgies came to an abrupt end when I rushed Susan to a hospital emergency room with terrible abdominal pain. She had surgery that next day to remove infected and damaged fallopian tubes, and ovaries full of endometriosis and cysts. A doctor later said that perhaps these complications were due to her early sexual activity and her two abortions at ages sixteen and twenty-one. After that she never smiled, and she shied away from any sexual contact. She suffered what was described as a "breakdown" and had to be medicated for clinical depression.

One day I received a call from the head of a local group called Adult Survivors of Incest. Susan's doctor referred her to this organization, and I was expected to take part in some of her therapy sessions. I learned that Susan's first pregnancy and abortion were the result of rape by her brothers and her father. Her father also had sex with her brothers while she watched! The ensuing letters and accusations within her family resulted in lawsuits. Through this nightmare of hatred, I was having an affair with one of her girlfriends and she was secretly seeing the local veterinarian. Our relationship crumbled and our marriage ended with my third divorce.

Oh, what a tangled web we weave, when first we practice to deceive ourselves.

Fast forward one year. I sold a million-dollar business and was promptly sued for nonperformance by the new owners. This resulted in a $1.4 million judgment against me. My daughter, Sylvia, was at fault when her car collided with a motorcycle, and I was slammed with a $400,000 excess liability judgment.

I decided to drown my troubles in a new environment. A friend and I purchased two Volkswagen Rabbits, loaded them with four television sets each, and drove from El Paso to Chapala, Mexico. We sold the TVs and the vehicles and lived on the interest from the proceeds. Chapala is a beautiful high desert resort area next to a large lake that sports a golf course and country club—and lots of rich residents.

I ended up with a huge case of hepatitis. I was so ill I had to return to the States and my daughter had to drop out of school to take care of me.

I was truly bankrupt—financially, morally, emotionally, and mentally. Suicide seemed like a perfect answer to end the chaos I had inflicted upon myself. I ate liver and onions and drank whiskey every day for three weeks. With my hepatitis, this diet should have killed me, but it didn't. Looking back, it seems kind of funny and kind of sad. Evidently God had a different plan for me.

Dale, my son by my first wife, came for a visit at Christmastime. Dale was twenty years old, and for the past year, he had been in a drug rehab program called Teen Challenge. The last time I saw him before he was sent there he looked like a homicidal maniac with crazed eyes and wild dirty hair. A doctor had told me to make arrangements to have him institutionalized for the rest of his life. Drug overdoses and the resulting mental illness had left him a violent schizophrenic.

He had been locked up in solitary confinement in a state hospital, but he beat up a guard and escaped. A Teen Challenge worker found him on the streets in Albuquerque and arranged for his referral to their rehab center in Tucson.

When Dale arrived and I opened the front door, I stared in amazement at a normal-looking young man. That afternoon as we sat at the kitchen table drinking coffee and visiting, it appeared to me that he had been miraculously healed. His mind and body seemed completely whole.

After I honestly described the misery of my own life, Dale told me, "Dad, you don't have to live like this. God loves you and has a plan for your life."

That night I thought about my son's incredible transformation. After I was in bed, I turned on the radio. A preacher named Skip Hietzig was talking about learning God's plan for your life. He said Jesus promised forgiveness for the chaos I had lived in and that my life could be like a new creation. He said Jesus Christ died for the entire body of sin in this world, including mine. I opened a Bible my mother had sent me for Christmas and began to read. Somehow God's message got through to me that night, and I surrendered my life to whatever God had for me. The rest, as they say, is history…and miraculous, as God touched and changed my life.

◆   ◆   ◆

I am writing my story on a computer not even invented twenty years ago when my child was sacrificed by abortion to hide my sinful life and to protect my financial assets. I named him Buddy, and I now know that he has forgiven me. I am comforted by God's Word that assures me that Buddy is safe in the arms of God.

The last time I heard from Susan, through her aunt, I learned she was married to a young Christian man and living in another state. Although childless, Susan was praising God for her new life, and her job as the head of their church's nursery program.

I married a lovely Christian widow in 1990 and helped to raise her daughter, who now has her own baby—my seventh grandchild. My son, Dale, has four children and is thriving in his own life. My daughter, Sylvia, although her mother got custody when we divorced, lived with me during her last two years of high school. After struggling as an abandoned single mom, Sylvia is married to a wonderful man and both she and her husband are public school teachers. She recently completed a master's degree and has two delightful, gifted children.

◆ ◆ ◆

I am on the board of directors of the local Pregnancy Crisis Center where we try to inject some sanity into the chaos surrounding crisis pregnancies. I speak with angry dads and granddads, as well as confused fathers-to-be.

I have had three heart attacks in three years. Six months ago my heart stopped for eight minutes. The last attack was just two weeks ago. But I'm still here. I now know two things for positive sure: One, there is a God who created all things, who is sovereign, and who is in control of all things. And two, Jesus Christ was *not* Plan B. Salvation from the Messiah was God's plan from the beginning of time so we could enjoy Him forever!

◆ ◆ ◆

You can see I have struggled with relationship commitments, sexual addictions, and situational ethics for many years. I regret that the consequences of my lifestyle were devastating, not only to me, but to many others along the way. I hope my story can help someone avoid the downward spiral with which I have had to deal.

—*Ernest Warren*

Editor's note: Teen Challenge, which helped Dale put his life back together, can be contacted at 1-417-862-6969 or online at www.TeenChallengeUSA.com.

Chapter Four

They Said I Was
Too Young to Have a Baby

My abortion happened around Easter just before I finished my freshman year of high school. I had been dating a guy who was a senior, and I couldn't believe this older guy would want to date me. I had stars in my eyes and would have laid my life down if he'd asked.

We slept together for the first time shortly after we met. Another guy had already taken my virginity, and I didn't realize that I could stop having sex anytime I wanted to. I thought it was normal for me to have sex with the person I was dating at the time and worried about what other people would think if I just suddenly stopped altogether. I wanted to appear mature. Wouldn't I look like a scared little girl if I stopped now?

After a couple of months, Jerry's feelings for me began to cool. Because my mom and dad were divorced, I vowed that I would make any relationship work that came my way. So I was devastated by his rejection. Shamelessly, I sobbed and begged him to come back, and for a while he did. But things were never quite the same. I always felt in danger of losing his love, always felt I had to do my best to stay prettier than the other girls or he might find someone else he liked better. I became anorexic to stay thin. Most nights were spent wondering why he hadn't called or where he was or who he was with, so I got very little sleep. Sometimes he would call at three in the morning. I would bolt out of bed to answer the phone so it would not wake up my dad. I lived and breathed this guy.

I wanted to get pregnant because Jerry's ex-girlfriend kept taunting me, claiming that she had had his baby and he was thinking of going back to her. I thought if I had his baby he would stay with me, and maybe he would start treating me better. I dreamed that we would be together forever. Jerry agreed we should have a baby, not realizing my ulterior motive.

We had been dating on and off for nine months, when I realized I was eight weeks pregnant. I was ecstatic but also scared. I was living with my dad and he had laid down the law: "You get pregnant and you're out of here." I understood what he meant. Getting pregnant would be crossing the line, and I'd be on my own to deal with it.

But I knew Jerry would protect me and our baby.

He told his parents, and we went to his house to meet with his mother and to talk about what we were going to do. We sat uneasily at the kitchen table listening to his mom. She declared that what was inside me was just a blob of tissue that didn't look anything like a human. I was naïve and knew very little about a developing baby. She insisted we had to get me an abortion as quick as possible before it got too big to abort.

"Jerry has a whole life ahead of him," she said. "You should be able to understand that he can't be tied down to you and a baby so early in his life." She said I was too young to be a good mother. Then, as though she thought I wasn't convinced, she threatened me: "If you give birth," she said, "we will get custody of the child so you will never see it again."

I was crying, and I looked at Jerry for support. He just slumped in his chair, staring at the floor. I knew his mom didn't like me, and I wouldn't put it past her to tell my dad. Finally, we talked about the cost of an abortion. I didn't have enough in my small savings account. She offered to lend me the rest of the money—but said I had to pay her back.

The whole idea of abortion panicked me. Never had the idea of killing my child crossed my mind. Not for a second. I was only fourteen, but I knew this was very wrong.

I had nowhere to turn, but I decided if my baby had to die, I would die, too. I tried to think of the least painful way to commit suicide. I could hang myself, but I didn't know how to tie a noose. I could turn on my dad's car and let it run in the garage, but I didn't know how to start a stick shift car. I didn't know anyone who owned a gun. I actually tried cutting my wrists, but there weren't any knives sharp enough and it hurt too much. I felt like a weak failure. I couldn't even kill myself!

The next week, I went to the school nurse. I asked her if she had to tell my folks if I came to her with something really bad. I wouldn't tell her my problem as I asked her over and over about whether it was legal for her to tell my parents. When she figured out I was pregnant, she admitted that, by the laws of our state, she was not required to tell my parents. She tried to persuade me to tell my dad, but I knew I couldn't. I remembered his warning. No. This had to be a secret.

The school nurse called the abortion clinic and made an appointment for Friday. We arranged for Jerry to take me to the clinic after my first-period class.

On Friday morning, I muffled my sobs in the shower. I jabbed my belly with my finger and called my baby a parasite, trying to distance myself from what I was about to do. My heart wasn't in those words, but I knew if I was going to do this, I had to do everything I could to keep my mind from envisioning a little face that would never be. I don't remember walking from gym class to the nurse's office or out to Jerry's car.

On the long drive to the clinic, I laid my seat all the way down so no one could see me and so I wouldn't be sick. We didn't speak the whole way, and I knew our relationship was over...this time, forever.

The clinic was in an old school building, which seemed sickly ironic. We drove past it once. There were no picketers or anyone trying to block the door. After we parked, a man on the sidewalk tried to talk to us, but Jerry yelled at him to leave us alone. We entered through a metal detector and up some stairs to the waiting room.

We waited for hours in a cramped room with about thirty other women. One woman sat next to me and declared loudly to her friend, "I already have one son. That's enough." It made me sad to think how callous these people were—workers and patients alike. I wanted so badly for some "crazed, lunatic Christians" to storm the doors and rescue me. But they didn't come.

I went into an office for a pregnancy test, and they confirmed that I was pregnant. A nurse told me it could be a tubal pregnancy, which would kill me, and how, because I was so young, I could die giving birth if I carried to term. I learned later that these statements were not true. I think this was a scare tactic so I would have the abortion.

When my name was finally called, I had trouble breathing and a pain in my throat made it impossible to swallow. I signed in and was sent back to the room where they do the suction abortions. I expected the doctor to be a nice person who would take pity on me. I asked if it would hurt and he said, "It's gonna hurt a lot more if you go through labor!" As he spoke, he didn't look directly at me, and he seemed irritated.

I felt like I didn't have a choice. My boyfriend wasn't going to let me leave until I went through with it. I couldn't go home and tell my dad. It would become obvious in a few months what was going on.

My baby's life ended that overcast April day.

On the way home, Jerry still didn't say anything. He dropped me at my house. I was alone. I tried to watch television but the screen was filled with images of children and babies, so I shut it off. I wanted to sleep but I couldn't go into my bedroom because I had already planned where my baby's crib would sit. I couldn't take a shower because I envisioned my baby playing in the tub. I just wanted to disappear, to not exist anymore.

In my junior year health class I found out that my baby had developed to the point of looking like a person with arms, legs, and a head. And she could feel pain. That knowledge will haunt me for the rest of my life.

My baby's name is Natalie, and she would have been born in November. She would be nine years old now, going into the fourth grade. I wonder sometimes, *Would she have been blond like me? Would she have liked to draw and paint?*

I would trade every success and milestone in my life to have her back. On this earth, I will never be able to hold her, kiss her goodnight, or tell her I'm sorry. I wish I had had the courage to stand up for Baby Natti.

◆   ◆   ◆

I now take full responsibility for the death of my child and for the denial that led to that tragic decision. I know that:

- I should have postponed having sex until I was married.
- I could have stopped having sex anytime I wanted to.
- Peers have less respect for someone who sleeps around than for someone who does not.
- Boyfriends and sex should not have been my outlet for grief over my parents' divorce; it only led to more destruction in my life.
- No guy is worth all the trouble I went through trying to keep a boyfriend who clearly didn't love me.

- The developing child inside me wasn't just a blob of tissue; she looked like a person from a very early stage.
- No one would have taken my child from me for being so young; that was a lie.
- My dad was just trying to scare me out of doing something stupid when he said he would kick me out of the house. He wept when he found out about my abortion.

◆ ◆ ◆

Through my tragedy Jesus touched my heart and came into my life as my Lord and Savior. Because I didn't end my life, I can now experience the goodness of God's grace. When I asked for His forgiveness, He not only forgave me but He gave me a clean slate. He remembers my sin no more. For that, I am eternally grateful! He's given me another chance at life even though I had created such a mess. My family knows about my abortion and we have been able to put that behind us. For that, I give God all the credit!

I am now married to a wonderful man who loves me and takes care of me. We have talked about starting a family, and I thank my Father in Heaven for mending my heart so I can look forward to having a baby and not feel ashamed.

◆ ◆ ◆

During the time I was writing my story, I discovered I was pregnant! We are so excited.

Natalie will always be my first baby; nothing will change that. But through the Lord's healing, I'm able to move on with my life and not dwell in my guilt and despair. I am "free indeed!" When I die, I know that God will welcome me into Heaven and standing next to Him will be my Baby Natti.

—Lisa Johnson

Chapter Five

My Husband Abused Me

Growing up on a ranch in central New Mexico, I lived out-doors—riding horses in the beautiful *piñon-* and juniper-covered mountains, working cattle, and helping my dad. My family worked hard, and we worked together. Driving the cattle to the railroad every fall to ship out the calves was the greatest fun of the year. My brothers and I whooped and hollered, slapping our chaps and acting like real cowboys as we galloped after strays. Daddy had the responsibility of getting the cattle to market without any of us getting hurt. Momma would cook and follow us in the pickup with whatever supplies we needed. It was a wonderful time.

Although we didn't have much money, we had the necessities, and my parents taught us the value of hard work and the satisfaction of a job well done. My parents gave me freedom: freedom to use my imagination, to explore, and to ponder things on my own. As a happy kid wanting to please everyone, I rarely got into trouble. After graduating from high school, I wanted to stay and work on the ranch, but my parents insisted that I go to college.

So I left my sheltered world. At New Mexico State University I wanted so badly to have friends and get involved in campus life. I met a few students in class but wasn't invited to any activities. I didn't realize I could meet more kids by joining a club or organization. There was even a Bridle Club to which ranch kids belonged. I continued to flounder socially, seeking a friendly face everywhere I went, and I was miserably homesick. Even though I made good grades, I hated school. I wanted to go home.

One day in class, a cute guy sitting next to me helped me solve a math problem. He offered to meet me the next day and give me some pointers on our homework. I was so excited; I finally had someone to talk to. Jason wore boots and a Stetson, so I was sure he must be a cowboy.

I knew Jason had a girlfriend, but I wasn't looking for a boyfriend, just a friend. One night after working on a math assignment at the library, he said, "There's a dance Saturday night. Wanna go?"

I hesitated. I knew his girlfriend, Katie. "What about Katie?"

"Things aren't so good with us. I think it's over."

Before long we were dating regularly. I met more people, went to dances, and was invited to parties.

But Jason was very possessive. He let other guys know that I belonged to him. I never had the chance to date other guys because they were afraid to ask me out. Afraid of Jason. I mistook his jealousy for love.

Several months later, we shuffled a two-step to *I'm a Honky Tonk Man* on the crowded dance floor at the VFW Hall. As I followed his lead between boot- and Wrangler-clad dancers, he asked me to marry him.

I said, "Yes." I was Cinderella twirling with my prince at the castle.

Looking back, I don't think I really loved him, but I hated school and his promises sounded so good.

Jason wanted to get married right away in Texas, where we wouldn't need parental signatures and there was no waiting period. The whole thing didn't seem right, so I put him off. My parents had no idea what was taking place. I didn't tell them about Jason; I was afraid they would be disappointed in me. I called home many times, begging my parents to let me come home. Every call ended the same: They insisted that I stay in school.

So Jason and I eloped. In the bathroom before the wedding ceremony, if there had been a window, I would have climbed out and run away. I cried through the entire ceremony. Within a month I was pregnant.

I knew Jason drank, but his drinking increased after we were married. When he drank, he became violent, pushing me and cursing me. After each terrifying episode he would be sorry and want to make up. As these frightful incidences continued, the attacks became more vicious. Once he pinned me against the bedroom wall and punched me in the chest, over and over. The beating fractured my collarbone and split my breastbone. I wore long sleeves to cover my injuries and made excuses when anyone noticed the many bruises.

One night at a western dance, Jason got plastered—falling down drunk. I asked his uncle, Harvey, to take him to his house, so we loaded Jason into the car and I helped dump him onto the bed at Harvey's before I went home. Jason's grandmother lived at Harvey's.

About an hour later, I watched headlights out the bedroom window as a car came down the dirt road to our mobile home. It was Harvey with Jason and Grandma. Jason fell out of the car and staggered toward the trailer yelling, "Come out here! I want to talk to you!"

I stepped out on the porch in my nightgown just as Grandma grabbed Jason's arm and tried to steer him back to the car. He slapped her across the face! She went down hard on the gravel drive, and he hit her two more times. Harvey grabbed him, and I screamed at him and tried to help Grandma. Jason jerked away and staggered into the house.

After Harvey and Grandma left, I finally mustered the courage to go inside. I stood in the doorway and listened. I could hear snoring from the bedroom. I stepped slowly into the living room willing the linoleum floor not to creak, crossed the room, and eased down onto the sofa. I sat there for the rest of the night…thinking…and praying that he would not wake up.

I was scared. If he would do that to his own grandmother, I realized he could kill me or hurt my unborn baby. About dawn, I finally knew what I had to do.

That morning I stood in the kitchen, keeping the table between us, not knowing what he would do. His bad breath roared across the table. He gulped down coffee without speaking and left, slamming the door behind him.

That night, as he watched a wrestling match on television, I told him I wanted a divorce. I was standing next to the door, in case I needed to make a quick escape. He reached over to the shotgun he kept next to his chair and patted it, as he said, "You're not going anywhere!"

The next day, when he left for work, I called a locksmith to change the door locks. The locksmith was a big guy, and I felt safe in case Jason returned. As he worked, I was in the bedroom feverishly stuffing Jason's things into plastic bags. As soon as the lock guy left, I dragged the bags of Jason's belongings onto the porch, locked the doors, and jumped into the car. It wasn't until I was miles away that I could breathe normally. I pulled onto the shoulder of the road and cried with relief. My plan was working. He couldn't get into the house. His stuff was out. And I was far away from the explosion I knew would happen when he came home.

For several days Jason called, trying to convince me to let him come home.

Later I learned that shortly after our wedding, Jason started spending time with his old girlfriend, Katie. She was pregnant and her baby was due one month after I was! After I locked him out of the house, Jason moved in with her.

As lonely as I was before I met Jason, I was even more lonely married to him. I finally realized there are a million things worse than being alone, and being married to a mean, bad-tempered, unfaithful person has got to be one of the worst.

I quit school and moved back to my parents' ranch before my baby was born. I loved being home, and the security of knowing I was safe from Jason's abuse. I was content with my life. The day I went into labor, Dad and I were throwing hay into overhead feeders for the cattle.

My daughter was, and still is, the light of my parents' life. Sara brought laughter and silliness to all of us. Dad couldn't wait for her to walk so he could take her with him to check the cattle and water tanks.

Sara and I lived with my parents for two years. Mom and Dad cared for Sara while I worked as a secretary, earning a small paycheck. Because of my lack of education and the fact that our town was small, I couldn't get a job that paid enough for us to live independently. I realized I needed to go back to school and committed myself to finishing college so I could provide a good living for my daughter and me. I packed our belongings and we moved to Portales.

After classes and on weekends, I took Sara with me as I worked a variety of part-time jobs. I painted corrals and pipe fences for a horse ranch and worked at a twenty-four-hour daycare center. During the summer and on school breaks, I helped Dad on the ranch. The most important thing to me, however, was that my daughter and I were together…and safe.

Then I met Manny. He had been raised on a ranch, he loved horses, and he was ambitious. Since he was a team roper, he was gone to rodeos most weekends. When he was in town, we dated. Eventually, we talked about getting married and moving to California where team roping was becoming a big-dollar rodeo event.

I dreamed about life with Manny and envisioned the perfect home for my daughter and a childhood for her much like my own. My self-esteem had bottomed out, and I was grateful that Manny could love me enough to want to marry me. Day-dreaming about our future made me feel more valuable.

The reality, however, was that it was only a pipe dream. In my mind I had created an image of Manny as a kind and loving person. Actually he was selfish and egotistical.

But one thing was startlingly real. I was pregnant! When I told Manny, his abrupt response was, "Get rid of it." He was going places and going to make it big. There wasn't room in our life for a baby.

I confided in a few friends. Their responses were similar. "People will think you're a slut." "It will be illegitimate." "You won't be able to finish college." "You'll never get a good job." From everyone I got the same advice: Have an abortion.

I went to a doctor's office and picked up literature on "choices." An abortion was described as a simple procedure…in and out in one afternoon…no complications…removal of tis-sue. So I decided to have the "procedure."

I drove myself to the clinic. I sat alone in the waiting room trying not to think about why I was there. After I went into the "procedure" room and was positioned on the cold table, I looked at the equipment in the room and wondered, *What in the world is all this stuff used for?* Surely, I thought, this "simple proce-dure" didn't require all those instruments.

A nurse strapped my feet into high stirrups, and it began. A doctor, who never spoke to me, forced what felt like the blunt end of a branding iron into my vagina so hard the pain caused my head to jerk backwards against the table. He shoved this metal rod in again, and again, and again. I could feel him scrap-ping inside my uterus. Noise exploded in my head! A roar like a loud vacuum sweeper. A sucking noise like a dentist's suction instrument. Slapping sounds like someone clapping their hands right next to my ear. I thought it would never end.

I screamed and begged them to stop! I shouted for help! But I wasn't making a sound; my pleadings were all inside my head. Tears soaked my hair and the table under my head. Finally, the doctor pulled the metal thing out and left the room.

A nurse took my feet out of the stirrups and helped me slide onto a padded gurney. She dried my face and washed the blood off my legs. She covered me with a warm blanket and let me rest a few minutes, and then she helped me get dressed. Before I walked out the back door, she gently hugged me and said, "Take care of yourself and don't come back here."

I've thought of the kind gestures by that nurse many times. Did she feel sorry for me? Did she have to do this job? Why did she stay there? These questions were never answered.

Numb and detached, I drove myself home. I collapsed on the bed. Everyone had been wrong. This was horrible. Everything felt wrong.

That night I thrashed around in bed; the whirling, sucking, slapping noises roaring in my head. When I did sleep, horrible, nightmarish dreams kept repeating themselves.

Then the crying started. A baby's cry. I checked Sara. She was sound asleep. I looked everywhere in our tiny apartment for the baby…in the bathroom, under the bed. Nothing! But the crying wouldn't stop. I realized there was no baby! I slumped to the floor next to my bed sobbing. Every night for months, the baby cried. How I wanted to comfort her. I thought I was going crazy. I asked myself a thousand times, "How could I have done such a thing? Why did I agree to have an abortion?" I was haunted by the thought that I could have taken care of another child, and that I should have at least given my baby a chance to live.

Manny and I dated off and on for six months. He never asked about the baby or the procedure. Even when I tried to tell him about the difficult time I was having, he showed no sign of concern or remorse. We finally split up.

◆ ◆ ◆

Eventually, I finished college when Sara was four years old. I met a wonderful man who loved Sara as if she were his own child. We talked about marriage, and I knew I had to tell him the truth about my past. When I told him about my abortion, Stanley cried tears of sorrow with me as he allowed me to mourn the death of my baby.

We married and Stanley wanted children. Three of them. Twice I got pregnant and twice I had miscarriages. My doctor said there was scar tissue in my uterus; there was no way I could carry a baby to term. He didn't say so, but I'm sure this damage was caused by my abortion. Now I've piled on more condemnation and guilt because I can't give my dear husband even one child. Eventually, I had to have a hysterectomy.

I successfully kept my abortion secret from everyone, only Stanley knew. Anytime I heard the word "abortion" I cringed and either left the room or changed the subject. If it came on television, I changed the channel. It was something I just could not handle.

Twenty-one years after my abortion, my husband and I were invited to a fundraiser for a local Pregnancy Crisis Center. I didn't know what the program would be, or I would not have attended. The whole program was about abortion! A speaker from Focus on the Family spoke about her abortion experience. She had written a book about how her abortion had affected her life, and about her pilgrimage in search of healing. As I listened, tears streamed down my face.

After the program I felt drawn to the table where the speaker was autographing books. I thought I'd buy a copy, take it home, secretly read it, and maybe it would help me. When I reached the book table, she stopped talking and turned directly to me. We chatted a few minutes before she picked up a book and handed it to me.

"You take this. I pray it will help you," she said.

How did she know? I wanted to run and I wanted to hug her, all at the same time.

I read the book, and then re-read it again and again. I called Focus on the Family and asked them to send me everything they had on post-abortion syndrome. My husband, God bless him, was extremely supportive and encouraged me to acquire as much information as possible.

I realized that I was not alone. As I came to understand that many women had suffered just like me and as I read about how they dealt with this trauma, I could feel healing beginning in my heart. As I got stronger, I knew I wanted to do what I could to help women understand how devastating an abortion could be. I called the local Pregnancy Crisis Center and asked how I could become involved. I shared with them about my abortion and found support and encouragement. They recommended that I tell trusted friends about my experience.

I confessed the abortion to my daughter and shared my grief with her. We cried together.

Twenty-four years after my abortion, I gave my testimony in church and shared the secret I had protected for so long. Finally, at long last, the paralyzing fear of someone finding out was quieted. After I spoke, several people asked for a recorded copy of my testimony so they could share it with someone they loved who had had an abortion.

I discovered that keeping the "secret" had actually interfered with my healing. This terrible secret took up so much room in my heart that it wouldn't allow the mending to begin that would put my broken heart back together.

I'm so thankful I have finally pulled loose from the clutches of my abortion and am healed from its horrors. But it took so many, many years.

I know that God has forgiven me and that my baby is secure in His loving arms.

—*Betty Jo Duncan*

Editor's note: Betty Jo contacted Focus on the Family at 1-800-A-Family.

Chapter Six

My Boyfriend Said, "If You Love Me, You Won't Force Me to Be a Father"

I joined the U.S. Air Force during Operations Desert Shield/ Desert Storm. I was twenty and excited to start new adventures living in northern Italy following K-9 police officer training.

Early one morning I was getting ready for my shift when the phone rang. The lady on the line said, "Can I speak with Al, please. This is his mother calling from Texas." I walked downstairs and knocked on the door of the room just below mine. I knew it was Al's quarters, even though we had never met.

After that brief meeting we were together constantly. I was smitten; it was love at first sight. I relished his attention. Our relationship was intimate, and physically and emotionally charged.

Two months later, I knew I was pregnant. Sitting in the hallway of my military barracks at two in the morning, praying no one could hear my voice, I dialed the number to Al's military post to tell him the pregnancy test results.

He simply responded, "Blue? It can't be blue."

For a while my pregnancy didn't seem real. I wasn't sick and my life wasn't affected. The people in my life proved to be less than supportive. My mother scolded me from halfway around the world saying, "What do you expect when you sleep with boys?" My girlfriends tried to guide me by sharing their stories of abortion. I didn't say it out loud, but I thought to myself, "Who are you trying to convince that abortion is okay, me or you?"

But most important to me was Al's attitude. He kept insisting I was forcing a life-altering experience upon him. He pleaded with me, "If you love me, you won't force me to be a father." He seemed threatened by the responsibility of fatherhood and his loss of freedom. I struggled to keep peace with the man I thought I couldn't live without.

I was confused about what to do and the military doctors were unsure as to how to handle my uncertainty. The treatment of women's healthcare issues was not well established and the military only provided basic medical care, since no hospital was available on base. All military personnel were sent to the local Italian hospital for specialty services including unwanted pregnancies. So I was provided with an appointment at the hospital and the name of the Italian doctor.

On the day of my appointment, Al and I walked down the stairs into the basement of the hospital. I held his hand so tightly I left fingernail marks in his palm. We sat on cold metal chairs beside several women lined up in a poorly lit corridor. I don't remember much about the appointment. After a brief conversation of broken English with a short doctor wearing a white lab coat, I was given a date and a time to be at the hospital. There was no discussion. No counseling. No mention of the word "abortion." Just a little white piece of paper with a date and a time.

The night before the procedure, a nurse led me to a long white room. Fifteen empty hospital beds lined the two walls separated by metal nightstands. The nurse said, "No visitors past eight o'clock," and left. I was alone until morning.

Shortly after dawn, my lonely room began to fill with Italian women who were also there to end their unwanted pregnancies. I endured awkward stares from these women as the nurses busied themselves preparing the patients. One nurse grabbed my feet, pointed to my toes, and fussed loudly at me in Italian. With a thick Italian accent, the woman in the next bed explained the nurse's outburst: "She's upset that you're wearing toenail polish."

As I watched the other women talking with those they had arrived with, I kept repeating my silent mantra, "Please don't let me go through this alone." The nurse had given me a shot, and I was dizzy—like I was being spun around on a merry-go-round. I wanted it to stop, but I couldn't get off. Then Al arrived. Wearing the same clothes as yesterday with dark circles under his eyes, his breath was heavy with the smell of liquor. He sternly threatened, "Stop crying or I'll leave." That's all he said.

One by one, the women were taken out of the room. Eventually it was my turn, and I was wheeled out the door, down the hall, into an elevator, and down to the surgical floor. As Al let go of my hand, he said, "I'll be here when you get back."

Placed alone in a hallway next to two large steel doors, I couldn't stop crying. I thought, *What am I doing? I can't do this!* People stared at me as they walked past. The metal doors banged open and a woman was wheeled out of the operating room, and I was quickly wheeled in. It was like an assembly line.

I was groggy from the sedative shot but I tried to tell everyone, "Wait! Wait! I'm not sure." I was still crying. No one understood and I couldn't speak Italian. One of the nurses said, "*Tranquilo. Tranquilo.*" ("Calm down.") She strapped my arm to the table and administered anesthesia. I focused on three large white lights above me as I shivered in the cold room and consoled myself by repeating, "Just go to sleep. Just go to sleep. Just go to sleep. It will all be over soon."

I awoke to my boyfriend's voice. "It's over with. Wake up." I curled into a fetal position attempting to ease the excruciating cramps and pain. "The nurses said the cramping should stop after a while," Al explained, as he attempted to comfort me. When the pain lessened, Al drove me to my barracks and I started medical leave.

Three days after the abortion, I spiked a temperature of 103 degrees and had unbearable abdominal cramping. Military doctors referred me to the same Italian doctor. Al helped me down the same stairs at the hospital to meet with the doctor. While doing a pelvic exam, the doctor held out his gloved hands to show me bloody mucous and tissue. He said, "I didn't get it all. I have to do it again."

I was devastated! In a daze and still in terrible pain, I dressed, walked out of the room, up the stairs, and out of the hospital. I sat in the car stunned and confused.

Al said, "What do you mean, he didn't get it all?"

In tears, I snapped back, "I have to go back because the tissue he left has caused an infection."

Back at the hospital that afternoon, I was placed in a small room with only two beds. My roommate was an American woman who had given birth that afternoon and was anxiously waiting for her baby to be brought to her. I could hear babies crying in the background. "Oh, no…I'm on the maternity ward." My roommate graciously offered to ask for another room and said, "I'm sorry for what you're going through. It must be tough seeing my baby."

The procedure was repeated the next morning, and I was hospitalized for four days as they administered drugs to combat the infection. I was discharged on a Sunday, and the next day Al flew out of Italy to an assignment stateside. Since then I have only seen him one time.

Because of continued problems in the year following the abortion, I was sent to a military hospital at Ramstein Air Base, Germany. A male doctor, a colonel, stood over me as I sat on the examination table and harshly said, "You should expect the pain. You had an abortion and these are the consequences. There's nothing I can do for you."

The following months and years were filled with promiscuity and searching for love and affection to fill the void of loneliness and heartache I felt. I struggled with depression, an eating disorder, and abusive relationships.

I saw Al three years after my abortion. When I attempted to share my sorrow and pain with him, he called me a liar. He mistakenly thought I was trying to renew our relationship by placing a guilt trip on him. All I wanted was closure.

◆ ◆ ◆

Four years after my abortion, a friend invited me to visit her church. After attending with her for several weeks, my life changed forever. At the end of the worship service on a Sunday I will never forget, the pastor asked everyone to bow in prayer and he said, "I've never done this before. We've never had an altar call, but I feel as though someone here today needs healing."

I knew he was talking about me. Any other time I would have been concerned about other people watching me or judging me, but this day was different. I rushed to the front as if I was being moved by something other than my own feet. The pastor grabbed my hand and said, "I knew you were going to come up here today." I burst into tears, oblivious to what anyone would think.

That day I shared my testimony…and I gave my life to God.

My commitment to God includes celibacy. I came to understand that intimacy and sex are gifts to be shared in the sanctity and holiness of marriage. I know now that every time I slept with someone, I gave a piece of myself away. A piece given here and a piece given there resulted in my being less than a whole person and certainly less than what God intended for me. But, praise God, He has made me whole again. Through God's word and forgiveness, I've learned the true meaning of love.

My abortion was the experience that broke my spirit and eventually brought me to God. For that I am grateful.

◆ ◆ ◆

I continue to have many health problems related to my uterus and cervix. I've had two additional surgeries to remove scar tissue and to help alleviate pain. Doctors are unsure of my ability to conceive a child, but I have faith that God will provide me with all that I need in His time.

> *For I know the plans that I have for you, declares the Lord, plans to prosper you and not to harm you, plans to give you hope and a future. (Jeremiah 29:11)*

Even after talking about my abortion many times, I still weep from the depths of my soul for the life of my child. I have experienced such incredible shame, guilt, sorrow, and heartache. Before my abortion, no one told me about these devastating consequences. Every woman I've spoken to who has had an abortion expresses deep sadness and grief for what she has done. The choice of abortion ends one life and destroys many others.

Looking back, I don't think I ever took the time to acknowledge and say to myself, "I'm carrying a life inside of me. I'm a mom. No matter what decision I make, *I am a mom!*" Abortion doesn't change this fact.

I'm convinced my baby was a girl and I have named her Alexis Reigh Yanez. She would be twelve years old. I know that someday I will hold her in Heaven.

—Pamela Engle

Chapter Seven

I Wanted a Quick Fix

At age eighteen in the 1960s, I was sexually active and terrified that my Catholic parents would find out. I got pregnant and the father was long gone. I didn't even know his last name. What was I supposed to do? I did two things. I got drunk, and I had an abortion. Seemed like good decisions at the time.

That abortion choice changed me forever and started me down a path of continued destructive behavior. For the next six years I indulged in drinking and promiscuity. I discovered some of those wonderful hippie drugs, and I started a deadly relationship with food and yo-yo dieting. I fell in and out of love a dozen times. During this chaotic time, I met the man of my dreams. He was perfect—almost. The one problem was that he was married. When we wound up pregnant, it seemed that there was only one easy choice—another abortion. I was so drunk the day of the abortion, the experience is a fog to me except for one feeling that has remained—a deep pain.

For the next eleven years, my life continued to spiral downward with more drinking, sex, and overeating. Two marriages ended in divorce. A pregnancy ended in a miscarriage.

As I look back on my life, I realize that God was always present trying to draw me to Him, but I wasn't paying attention. I had abandoned my Catholic faith in my college days. At age thirty-one God blessed me with a son, and four years later

God gave me the gift of sobriety. My sobriety started my journey back to God and eventually back to my Catholic faith.

When my son was ten, my married boyfriend and I were pregnant again. This time I was sober. This time I wanted to keep the baby. But he gave me a choice—the baby or him. I wonder how I could have cared for this man who obviously did not want what was best for me. I was angry and hurt, but after so many years of craziness and foggy thinking, I caved in and had my third abortion.

For all these years, I had been passionately pro choice. Then one autumn day three years ago, I didn't have transportation to my regular church for Sunday Mass, so I went to a church closer to home. After Mass I picked up a church bulletin that contained a small advertisement about Rachel's Vineyard post-abortion retreats and a website address. Being a computer junkie, as soon as I got home I jumped online to the website. As I read their information, I sobbed. Tears streamed down my cheeks as I realized that it was time for me to deal with my abortions.

Last year, I finally attended my Rachel's Vineyard Retreat. There are no words to adequately describe this profound experience. I was shown how to look at my abortions through new eyes. This was the first time I had ever told anyone about this part of my life. I shared my experiences with other post-abortive women. Their acceptance and love helped me to begin my healing.

I faced my three aborted children and named them Luke, Grace, and Benjamin. I asked each of them for their forgiveness. I also named the child I miscarried, Teresa. She, too, has a special place in my heart. Through the miracles of this weekend retreat I know that God has forgiven me, and I am on my way to forgiving myself. Thirty-six years of denial, shame, guilt, pain, sadness, and anger began melting away as the healing process began.

At my retreat, I made this promise to my aborted children:

I promise you that I will no longer be silent about you. I will not hide in shame or guilt. I commit to turning our pain and sorrow into something good and positive. I will find a way to honor your existence and your deaths. I will let Jesus guide me in memory of you.

I have discovered many ways of keeping this promise. First, I shared my story with my family. Each family member was unbelievably caring, loving, and supportive. I am blessed; not all post-abortive women get such positive, compassionate responses.

After the retreat I was delighted to discover that I could use my God-given talents for writing and speaking to keep my promise to my children, and to help others understand the devastating aftermath of abortion. So I am writing articles, writing letters to newspaper editors, and telling my story at every opportunity.

A month after my retreat, I walked in a Memorial Day parade in memory of Luke, Grace, and Benjamin, humbly wearing a T-shirt printed with the words, "Women Regret Abortion." Since my retreat, I am a changed person. I share my story openly, no longer hiding in silence and burdened by guilt and shame.

How did this happen? A metaphor for the process I'm going through dawned on me one day during my morning prayers. At age eighteen, I was a whole, beautiful mirror. That mirror was shattered into a million pieces when I had my first abortion. I arrived at my Rachel's Vineyard Retreat, with my life as broken as that mirror. I brought all those pieces of glass to my retreat—the painful splinters that were wounding me spiritually, emotionally, and physically. By attending the retreat, I was finally acknowledging how broken I was. The mercy and love of Christ helped me to name and acknowledge my wounds.

At the retreat, Christ gave me a picture frame for the broken pieces of glass, and I began to put the pieces of my mirror back together inside that frame. The early part of the process was really painful. I had to pull all those sharp slivers of glass out of my soul and look at them. This was hard and painful work, but with Christ's love all around me, comforting me and guiding me, I was able to do it.

I returned home from the retreat and continued the process of fitting those broken shards inside the frame of Christ's love. It is slow work, but Christ's forgiveness and mercy hold all those pieces in place.

As I lay my brokenness at the feet of Christ, He has allowed me to honor the promise that I made to my children. As I speak out, through my voice or my pen, another piece of my shame and guilt is fit back into the almost complete mirror.

Another part of my renewal is what my wonderful retreat facilitator calls "interior work." She recently reminded me, "There are many quiet, personal, slow, interior steps which must be made, too. These are the deep ones, which knit you together and make you into a garment of warmth and safety for spreading God's love and forgiveness onto others."

This quiet, prayerful work is hard for me; I am so accustomed to living with blaring external noises. Although silence is difficult, I'm making a concerted effort to do this "interior work."

The mirror is almost complete, and the reflection I see today is of a woman forgiven and free. I see a woman who is:

- Free of the shame, the guilt, the self-torture, and the self-loathing that I carried for so many years
- Free from many of my destructive behaviors and habits
- Free to love more openly
- Free to listen, to learn, and to speak my truth

- Free to love my living son in new and glorious ways, and to be a better mother to him

My abortions did change me forever and my mirror will never be perfectly whole again. But even with some missing pieces and cracks, I am more beautiful today than ever. What a blessed journey!

Thank you, Jesus! And thank you, Holy Spirit, for guiding my pen as I let other post-abortive women know that they are not alone, and that in Christ there is healing and forgiveness for them, too.

—Susan Swander

Editor's note: The website that led Susan to her retreat is www.RachelsVineyard.org.

Chapter Eight

I Wish Someone Had Told Me…

I wish someone had told me…
- That the first time I had sex, I would get pregnant.
- That the "man" with whom I shared that first intimate moment would choose not to father his child.
- That the "man" who seemed to know what was best would actually be encouraging me to make the most regretful decision of my life, as well as his.
- That $300, the cost of my abortion, would not fix my problem, but instead would cause more emotional and physical trauma than I could possibly imagine…and would ultimately change my life forever.
- That my choice was motivated by feelings of shock and fear, by my being self-seeking and irresponsible, and by worry about what my parents, friends, and family might think.
- That there were people who would have loved to adopt and cherish my child.
- That there were agencies that would help me, if I had decided to parent or place my baby for adoption.
- That my parents might have understood if I had told them I was pregnant.
- Not to make a rash decision based on the influence of others…or on my university scholarship.
- That my life didn't have to stop because I was pregnant.

- That other options were available.
- That life is about choices, and this "pro-choice" decision I was making would result in a truly "poor choice."
- That there was at least one person who would be willing to help me.

I wish someone had told me...
- That the abortion clinic's staff would humiliate me.
- That neither Planned Parenthood nor Family Planning would know the first thing about caring for their clients.
- That the girl ahead of me in line would laugh the whole time, claiming her fifth abortion, and declaring, "It's easy, not to worry."
- That I **could have** gotten off of the table, when I realized I was making a horrific mistake.
- That I could have changed my mind until the very last minute, no matter what the doctors or nurses told me.
- That a part of my maternity would die on that table, right along with my child.
- That I would feel more appalled with myself after the "procedure," as I was ushered out the clinic's back door.
- That people didn't talk about these "kinds of things," that after "it" was over, I wouldn't be able to talk about it either.
- That there would be so much physical and emotional pain involved...not just then, but twenty-three years later.
- That I would lose a part of my dignity, self-love, and purpose in life.
- That one day I would deeply regret this "choice."

I wish someone had told me...
- That I wasn't God and that He alone should determine life and death.

I wish someone had told me...
- That the emotions of grief, guilt, and shame would take over my life.

- That for years I would wake up crying in the middle of the night.
- That due to the emotional pain of my "choice," I would consider suicide twice.

I wish someone had told me...
- That a baby is always a gift and miracle.
- That the description of my fetus being "just a blob of tissue" would be understood as dishonest when I graduated with a double degree in child development and psychology.
- That seven years later, the joy of seeing my son's ultrasound pictures would be tainted by sorrow, knowing that I had terminated my first child's life.
- That the birth of my son would truly be a day of reckoning for me.
- That my son's hugs and kisses, or hearing him say, "I love you, Mommy, more than all the houses, stars, and cars!" would mean more to me than I can possibly explain; that my aborted son might have shared similar "endearments."
- That two years after my marriage, my husband and I would be separated and seeing a marriage counselor.

I wish someone had told me...
- That while visiting a friend's house, I would be a victim of nonconsenting sex.
- That I would get pregnant from that situation.
- That I might be forced to choose abortion again, because those closest to me said I couldn't bring a biracial child into the world, while I was married to someone else.
- That abortion wouldn't save my marriage.
- That I would be divorced five years later, after my husband became involved with my best friend.
- That on the anniversary dates of my abortions and on the due dates of my babies, I would feel numb and unable to move.

I wish someone had told me…
- That later I would miscarry another pregnancy and never be able to have other children.
- That I would have a hysterectomy before I was forty years old.

I wish someone had told me…
- That at age thirty-eight when I became a Christian, my heart's wound would reopen and ache even more for my two aborted babies.
- That I would again weep for those children, even though I knew they were in heaven.
- That when I finally chose to admit my sin, I would be told, "Just forget about it" or "It was your choice."
- That people wouldn't let me talk about it, and would judge me. even the people who call themselves "Christians."

I wish someone had told me…
- That it would take the accepting hearts and compassion of a few select women to assist in my healing.
- That I would eventually find others who had suffered in silence.
- That I could go through a healing program in which God would release me from the shame, guilt, and grief that I had suffered for so many, many years.

◆ ◆ ◆

I'm glad someone told me…
- That God had personally carried my children home to Heaven!
- That God has wanted to comfort me!
- That I could name my children, who are forever covered with His fingerprints!
- That Dylan Conor and Dory Kalani could be close to me in heart and soul, even here on earth!

- That the process of forgiving myself would be terribly painful and tearfully emotional, yet divinely possible!
- That on the cross, Jesus did all that was needed for my sins to be forgiven!
- That when I finally get to Heaven, Dylan and Dory won't remember why I haven't held them, hugged them, or kissed them!
- That God's grace would set me free!

◆ ◆ ◆

I'm glad to be able to tell you…
- That my hurts have been made into halos, and beauty has been made of ashes!
- That God has allowed me to comfort others, as He comforted me and held my hand during my own recovery!
- That I have been blessed to talk about my unborn children to high school and college students, to church congregations, at fundraisers, during awareness campaigns, and to my own son!
- That I honestly shared my own sins with my son, and that he committed his life to Christ and to "life" itself!
- That God truly is the most amazing, awesome, forgiving, loving Father any person could ever know!

◆ ◆ ◆

I'm glad someone told me…
- To share my story with you!

—Stacy Lynn Massey

Editor's note: Stacy is president and cofounder of Abortion Recovery International Network and the founder of Abortion Recovery Counseling, Education & Outreach. These organizations are listed in the Appendix.

Chapter Nine

I Had Just Begun My Career

I was nineteen years old and living with my boyfriend, Vince. I had just started working as a hairdresser in a beautiful salon, and I loved the creative nature of my work.

One day I realized my period was late. That afternoon after work I bought a pregnancy test. The next morning I woke up really early and did the test with a urine sample. I left the test strip on the counter and sat on my bed waiting, looking into the bathroom, counting every second…anxious but not really wanting to know. Finally, I peeked through the door. The color was evident even before I saw the test results. Positive! Oh, no!

I stumbled back to the bed and sat in shock. Immediately, I thought, "I have to have an abortion." Vince was out of town, and I called him in tears. How I wish he had been there. I needed him to hold me—to be my support. I felt so alone!

Vince agreed with my abortion decision and three weeks late he drove me to the abortion clinic. As we pulled into the parking lot, a man approached and handed Vince some literature through his car window. Then I saw the man was carrying a poster with a photo of a baby, I screamed at my boyfriend, "Noooo, keep driving!" Until then I had held myself together pretty well, but at the sight of that baby, I couldn't hold back the tears.

We got inside to a waiting room. I couldn't stop crying. I realize now I was looking for help. I was looking for someone to say, "You can have this baby, and it will be okay."

When they called my name I went into a back room. I was shocked at how many girls were there! Some were very young, and each one looked sad and frightened. I still couldn't stop crying, and I had difficulty breathing.

A nurse took me out of the room and sat me in an office across the desk from a rather stern-looking woman in a nurse's uniform. She looked over her glasses at me and said, "You don't seem like you really want to do this. Are you sure about this?"

I told her, "My mom will kill me if she finds out, and I'm afraid because I've started doing some drugs."

She just said, "Okay," and instructed me to go back into the holding room. From there I was shuttled in and out for blood tests and urine specimens and exams—for two hours.

In one room I was put on a table with stirrups before the doctor breezed in. When he tried to examine me, I couldn't keep still on the table. He rose to his feet, glared at me over my knees, and yelled at me. "If you don't spread your legs, you won't get this abortion." I started to cry again. His treatment was so shocking and devastating; I knew I had to leave. But I didn't. When I look back on this, I realize that had been my opportunity to walk out and allow my baby to live.

Finally, I ended up on a gurney in a room with four other girls separated only by a curtain hanging on silver rings from the ceiling. A nurse came in, examined me, and said, "You're eleven weeks." Then she moved quickly to the girl behind the next curtain.

They next rolled me out into the hallway. I was still crying. A doctor stopped next to me, leaned down, and whispered, "Dear, if you continue to cry like this, you will hurt much more after the surgery." Though that doesn't seem very caring, it was the warmest touch I had had. I nodded my head and bit my lip trying to stifle the sobs.

When they rolled me into the prep room, they placed me next to a beautiful girl. We didn't talk, but I looked over at her and watched a tear roll back on her face. Then they took her away. I knew I was next! It seemed like only minutes, and they came and got me. They rolled me into a cold, very white room. Everyone there wore white. I was scared and stiff, it felt so cold. The anesthesiologist leaned over me, put the mask on my face, and told me to count from ten to one. "Ten...nine...eight...."

I woke up on my stomach and in pain. I felt empty and alone. I knew my precious baby was no longer inside of me.

After that, my relationship with Vince was strained and I moved out.

Then I got pregnant again. I didn't know what to do. The father of the baby didn't know what else to do either, so he gave me the money to have an abortion. I don't remember making the appointment. On the scheduled day, my roommate, who was a good friend and who was very protective, took me and held my arm as she walked me past some demonstrators outside the clinic.

She helped me fill out the paperwork and sat with me until my name was called. It all seemed familiar—the waiting room full of girls, the exams, the blood tests. But I was numb. It was as though a callus had formed on my heart. Although the process was familiar and the pain was familiar; the emptiness afterward felt far deeper.

I tried to cover my heartache with drugs and alcohol. A few lines of cocaine would deaden the pain—for a while. I became addicted to cocaine. I drank and partied and smoked, searching for relief from the emptiness. This continued for almost ten years.

During this time my dear brother, Chris, was brokenhearted and mad at me as he watched me destroying myself. One day he angrily told me, "Lisa, you are no longer my sister! You are going to die if you don't stop doing this to yourself!"

His angry outburst stunned me. We had always been so close. This was the little brother who would run into my room at night during a thunderstorm. This was the brother who had taught me how to swim and how to throw a baseball. I loved him dearly. I cried all night.

The next day Chris called and apologized. He said he had spoken out of fear and concern. Then he said, "I just want you to get your life back." I thought: *What's wrong with my life? It's full of fun and friends.*

But I knew that Chris had a joy and peace in his life that I didn't have. He was a Christian, and one day I agreed to go to church with him. I wanted to see if his Jesus was so much different from the one I thought I knew. He took me to Calvary Chapel in Costa Mesa. During the sermon, the pastor said that Jesus Christ loved everyone. *Me?* He said that, no matter what a person's sin was, that Jesus was willing to forgive and to wash that person clean. *Even the terrible things I've done?* The pastor said if anyone wanted a personal relationship with Jesus Christ all he or she had to do was ask. *Even me?*

After the sermon, the pastor said, "If anyone wants to ask Jesus to be your Lord and Savior and Friend, and if you want your sins forgiven, come forward now. I want to pray with you." *Jesus couldn't possibly forgive me.* But the possibility sounded so inviting.

In the next few days, I thought of nothing else. Imagine a chance to start over. Was it possible? Later that week, I talked with my brother and told him that I wanted to walk forward at the next church service. I wanted to see if God would make all of this pain in my heart go away. Would He really forgive me?

My entire family anxiously joined us the next week and watched me walk forward and ask Jesus into my heart to be the Lord and Savior of my life.

Since that time my life has truly changed. It is nothing less than a miracle. First God helped me break my drug addiction. Then I kicked the alcohol addiction. Then the promiscuity. Then the cigarette habit. And the process isn't finished; I'm still being changed. Every step with Jesus is so much more rewarding than any of the wrong steps I took on my own.

Although I think often about my babies, Vincent and Alicia, God has freed me from the pain and guilt of my abortions. Abortion didn't make my babies "go away"; they will live in my heart forever. I do wonder where these precious children would be today if I had not made those wrong choices, but the emptiness in my heart is gone. I know I will see them again in heaven, and I am comforted by the fact that Vincent and Alicia know nothing but the love of our Savior, Jesus Christ.

◆ ◆ ◆

I am now married to a wonderful, godly man who honored me before marriage. Stan had made a vow of sexual purity and he saved himself until marriage. I am so thankful God had washed me clean of all my past sexual sins, and when I became a Christian He allowed me to also make a vow of purity and save myself for my husband. Stan was certainly worth the wait, and I adore him with everything that is in me.

Sadly, I have not been able to get pregnant even though we would love to have children. But God is so good. Recently I met a beautiful young lady in a crisis pregnancy. I was privileged to help her see that abortion was not a good choice, and I rejoiced when she chose life for her baby. Shortly after our first meeting, she asked me if my husband and I would adopt her baby. We have accepted her loving and generous offer, and we wait with a great anticipation for this baby with whom God has chosen to bless us.

◆　◆　◆

I have learned that I must forgive as I have been forgiven. It would be easy to stay angry at the people who failed me, that should have helped me make better choices. But I know that anger and bitterness toward others only hurt me. God has given me the ability to forgive and forget.

I now understand that the path of drugs and alcohol and promiscuity that I traveled, trying to ease the pain and guilt from my abortions, was destructive. I only wish I had turned to God earlier; I could have saved myself and my family so much grief. I still marvel at the magnificent way He has cleaned out the pain and bitterness and grief. If He will do this for me, He will do it for anyone who is hurting from an abortion.

◆　◆　◆

It has not been easy to write my story. But I rejoice that I have had the opportunity for the last ten years to tell my story and help other women avoid the wrong choices I made and the devastating consequences I suffered.

I also have been able to minister to hurting post-abortive women and share the love, healing, and forgiveness that the Lord provides.

I will be forever grateful that God showed me His love and His forgiveness. Because of the blood that Jesus shed, I am cleansed from my sin, from my shame, and from my sorrow.

—Lisa Musil

Chapter Ten

I Had No One to Talk To

This testimony was difficult to write and painful to read. But the act of writing it was very healing for me. As you read it you might wonder, "Why would she be willing to share her shame and disgrace in such intimate detail?" The answer is simple: because of Grace. At the Lord's leading, I am using my real name as a bold demonstration as to the power of His Grace. Grace is real. And Grace is very powerful.

I hope this story of my past can be used to change the future.

I Never Thought It Would Happen to Me

At age twenty-six, I had a college degree, a career in management, and had recently become a Christian. On the outside I looked good, but I wasn't okay. I was plagued with an eating disorder and a problem with alcohol. I knew my boyfriend didn't love me; our relationship was unhealthy, even abusive. And I was single and pregnant.

There was no one to talk to or turn to. I was a loner and didn't have any close friends, and I hadn't talked to my parents for six years. While I still lived with them, I had attempted suicide. After that, my relationship with my folks cratered, and I moved out. I was considered the proverbial "black sheep" of the family.

I didn't allow myself to consider any option except abortion. Emotionally, I was bankrupt in so many ways and barely surviving. At the end of my rope, I had no one I could trust. It was a very bad time.

I didn't know much about abortion, although I had read a few newspaper articles about it. I thought of abortion as a lofty debate about morals, between passionate pro-life and pro-choice people—an argument I thought would never be resolved. I assumed it only affected high school girls. I ignorantly assumed abortion was illegal, and I considered it immoral.

The Beginning of the End

Since my menstrual cycle was always as regular as clockwork, I became alarmed when I was two days late. I dashed to the drugstore and bought an over-the-counter pregnancy test. The result—positive! I was petrified with fear, overwhelming shame, and looming disgrace. From that point on I was like a robot, never looking to either side at other options, only straight ahead toward abortion. To me it was as though my only other option was suicide.

That night, unable to sleep in the wee hours of the morning, I sat up in bed and flipped on the television. Surfing the channels, I stopped on a movie called *The Silent Scream*. It was an ugly and disturbing film showing the actual abortion of a twelve-week-old child. I cringed at the ultrasound pictures, and it distressed me to see the baby thrash about. I shut the TV off before the end, fearful that I might be swayed to change my mind about my abortion choice. I couldn't allow that to happen.

As upsetting as the pictures were, I convinced myself they had nothing to do with my own situation since I was only three days late—still just a few cells, not a baby like the one on the TV screen.

Before dawn I drove to the photo-finishing lab I managed. It was still very dark, and I bought a newspaper at a 24-hour convenience store. Seated at my desk I spread the paper open to the classified ads and scanned the columns for an abortion clinic. Even though I wouldn't allow myself to consider that I was carrying a baby, I knew deep in my heart that what I was doing was wrong and so my plans needed to be done in secret and under the cover of darkness.

The descriptions I had heard, "It's only a blob" and "It's just a few cells," reinforced my denial. I chose to believe I still had a "choice," even though I was pregnant. Pro-choice slogans like "Women have rights and choices!" and "An untimely pregnancy can ruin a woman's career!" were hedging me in and giving me the courage to abort.

Among the abortion clinic classifieds was an ad for an organization I knew was not an abortion clinic. I can't say why I called that number, but I did. Perhaps I possessed the slightest hope that maybe someone, somewhere, would help me. I waited anxiously as the phone rang and rang. Finally, an answering machine picked up. An enthusiastic-sounding man spoke very quickly, like he was desperate. The way he spoke alarmed me. I couldn't afford to feel desperate.

The voice urged that if it was an emergency to call another number, and I quickly jotted it down. The word "emergency" made me uncomfortable. What if I allowed myself to admit this was an emergency? How could I take refuge in my "choices," if I acknowledged that something was at stake or in danger? I looked at my watch, then at the phone number. I didn't have the courage to wake up a stranger, and I couldn't wait for sunrise. I needed immediate resolution. I mustered all my energy to stay calm and focused. I had rights and choices. It was still dark outside, and I was safe.

I dialed the number of a nearby abortion clinic just as two of my employees wandered in and were chatting while they waited for coffee to brew. Even at that early hour, a person at the clinic answered the phone. She sounded businesslike, and I was relieved to actually have a real person to talk to who was kind and calm and not alarmed by my call.

That afternoon as I drove to the clinic; the clear, sunny spring day contrasted with the way that I felt. I wished it were cloudy and still dark, yet the warmth of the sunshine felt somehow comforting.

The Abortion Clinic

The outer waiting room was filled with anxious-looking boyfriends, girlfriends, sisters, and moms. I was told to go directly into another waiting room, where I was quickly checked in.

I was handed a medical form on a clipboard and told to fill it out. The blurred form had been copied so many times it was hard to read and one corner was clearly missing. As I sat at the end of the nurse's desk, I noticed there were about thirty pieces of white adhesive medical tape neatly lined up in a long row with a corner of each piece stuck to the shelf. After I gave the form back to the receptionist, she pulled a piece of tape off the shelf, stuck it to the metal clip on my board, and wrote my name on it. She then slipped a manila file folder under my medical form. My name was written on the tab on top of so many layers of white-out that it cracked when I bent it.

The many pieces of tape hanging from the shelf made me feel better; I was not the only one doing what I was doing. Now, years later, all I can think about is how each piece of tape represented a baby.

Next I was sent to a restroom with instructions to put my clothing in a cubbyhole and to come out in a hospital gown. All the cubby spaces were filled, so I rolled my clothing into a ball, and placed it in a corner on the floor.

In a small room, a doctor gave me a quick exam and said that I was at least six weeks pregnant. I knew that couldn't be true, but I didn't say anything. The doctor was kind and friendly, although rushed. He said it was no big deal, and that soon I wouldn't have a problem anymore. He didn't ask if I had any questions.

The Long, Narrow Room

After the exam I was ushered to a chair at the end of a long, narrow waiting room. Both sides of the room were lined with about twenty women sitting in hospital gowns or bathrobes. I sat down quickly and didn't make eye contact with anyone.

I listened as the other women nervously discussed their situations. A doe-eyed high school student whispered, "I don't really want to do this. My parents are making me. My dad is over the top about this pregnancy, and I have to keep the peace for my mom's sake."

A slender college graduate apologetically added, "I've worked so hard in school and I only graduated a few months ago. I got a great job in New York, and I don't want to give it up."
An older woman quietly wept as she rubbed her abdomen and explained, "My husband absolutely doesn't want any more kids. I don't want to do this, but I don't want to lose him. I have to do it, to save my marriage."

A heavy door at the other end of the long room opened and we all jumped. The woman closest to the door got up and went in. The door banged shut. A woman with dark curly hair was wringing her hands and nervously wondered out loud if having an abortion would keep her from having children in the future. A college student wearing a thick bathrobe and fuzzy slippers and clutching a teddy bear reassured her, "This is my third abortion at this same clinic. Don't worry, there will be other pregnancies." Even though we were all in the same boat, everyone gasped in shock at her proclamation.

Studying the row of patients on the other side of the room, I thought about how none of them looked pregnant. The conversation turned to the subject of the protesters who had lined the sidewalk outside the clinic. The older woman who was fearful of losing her husband said, "That man spouting Bible verses made me feel terrible." With tears in her eyes she continued, "What? Did they think we came to this decision lightly?"

I was grateful I hadn't seen any protesters; I guessed that was because I had been the last one to come in.

The door opened again and another woman was gone.

All was quiet for a time, and then several talked about who had brought them and who was waiting to drive them home. The woman across from me looked at me and asked who had brought me. "No one," I replied, "I came on my own." My remarks seemed to strike a collective nerve. Of all of the sad stories shared in that long room, my statement seemed to evoke the most sympathy. The reason for this, I believe, was because we all understood we were there to destroy a part of ourselves, but each of them at least had someone with them to help deal with the pain and loss. I felt their pity. I was glad when the door opened again, distracting everyone; I was uncomfortable with the unwanted attention.

Eventually, I was the only one left. I knew the next time the door opened, it would be my turn. An intense wave of exhaustion swept over me. I closed my eyes and waited.

Behind the Big Door

The room where the abortion was performed looked like any regular ob/gyn office, and I was quickly anesthetized. The next thing I remember was the room swimming, and I was being helped off a stretcher and into a recliner chair in another room. Several women silently watched as I was given a very large tablet for the pain and told that I would have abdominal cramping for the next twenty-four hours.

The staff was anxious to go home and although I was still very groggy, I concentrated hard on gaining my bearings and getting dressed. Although I was not completely alert, I drove myself home.

I went on with life and tried to pretend, unsuccessfully, that the pregnancy and abortion never happened. Although pro-choice slogans gave me the courage to choose abortion, there was no comfort for the pain, suffering, and confusion that followed. I was faced with the harsh reality that I had done something horrible and that it could not be undone.

I was a new Christian, but I believed my sin was too great for Christ's forgiveness and I attempted suicide. The Lord intervened in the attempt to end my life and from that point on I pursued a relationship with Him with an intense, fiery passion and complete abandon. I turned my back on the ways of the world and threw myself into studying God's Word, and prayer, and fellowship with other Christians. During that time the Lord healed the relationship with my family.

Grace: The Path to Healing

There were still great challenges to my healing in the area of post-abortion regret.

Two years later the Lord blessed me with a wonderfully loving, godly husband. When I gave birth to our first son, I was overwhelmed with powerful feelings of love for him. Until then I had never known "the love of a mother." Staring in amazement at our beautiful son, I painfully remembered the child I had aborted.

We now have three amazingly beautiful children. Loving our children as much as I do, I cannot begin to imagine not having one of them. It is beyond my ability to even ponder. However, there is currently an empty seat in my minivan, which would not be empty, had I not exercised my "choice." There could have been another wonderful child sitting in that seat or in our pew at church.

This reminder and countless others require daily access to God's Grace. If God's Grace were not real or very powerful these reminders would be too much to bear.

Ten years following my abortion I attended a women's retreat and met a woman who became a trusted friend and prayer partner. She was the director of the ABC Women's Center in Middletown, Connecticut. I would review post-abortion study guides for use at the center and after several years, she asked me to apply for the board of directors. These activities were very helpful in my own healing.

This healing was a slow process because it took me years to fully comprehend the consequences of my abortion decision. It was painful and scary because I had to first admit that I had destroyed my child. It brought me back to the Garden of Eden and the desire to blame others because of the lies I had heard and believed. Lies or no lies, I had to admit to my responsibility so I could ask forgiveness, and receive God's immediate reply, which is and always will be, Grace. My complete healing took thirteen years.

Our Battle Is Not Against Flesh and Blood

My husband and I vote pro-life; we participate in peaceful pro-life marches, and pray for legislative change. However, we do not believe these efforts will bring victory over abortion. This battle is too enormous to fight with bumper stickers, slogans, demonstrations, campaigns, and even legislation.

I believed abortion to be illegal. No one pressured me. I watched *The Silent Scream* the night before. I called a pro-life organization the morning of. I knew that what I was doing was wrong. I saw the condemnation caused by the pro-life protesters on the faces of the women at the abortion clinic. And I was a Christian.

Yet I still chose abortion. Why? Because this is a spiritual battle!

> *For our struggle is not against flesh and blood, but against the rulers, against the authorities, against the powers of this dark world and against the spiritual forces of evil in the heavenly realms. (Ephesians 6:12)*

> *He (the devil) was a murderer from the beginning, not holding to the truth, for there is no truth in him. When he lies, he speaks his native language, for he is a liar and the father of lies. (John 8:44b)*

Satan's plan of attack through abortion is devastatingly well designed to destroy mother, child, family, honor, respect, and sanctity of life.

A Chorus of Confirmation

As I typed this testimony, a chorus swirled inside my head:

> *You have given me the oil of gladness,*
> *a garment of praise instead of mourning,*
> *a shining crown instead of ashes*
> *and glory in the place of despair.*

That chorus is based on chapter 61 in the Book of Isaiah. The verses of this chapter contain a calling, anointed by the Holy Spirit, to release the prisoners from darkness. It says, "He has sent me to bind up the brokenhearted…to comfort all who mourn."

My God has not cursed me; He has blessed me! He has not condemned me; He has forgiven me! He has not forsaken me; He calls me, and anoints me, and loves me with an everlasting love that is beyond my comprehension!

The blessings of Isaiah 61 are not only for me, but also for all who would receive them in Christ Jesus. We have access to glory in the place of despair!

A Garment of Praise to Replace a Veil of Shame

The Lord's heart is for the hurting to be healed! Beloved, if you suffer from post-abortive regret, please respond to the Lord's invitation to receive His healing touch. You don't have to live with the pain, shame, and condemnation. A wonderful door is open for you. The door is called "Grace." The Lord wants to heal your hurt and to give you a garment of praise to replace your veil of shame. God's son died so that you don't have to continue suffering. His forgiveness sets you free and allows you to live in the abundance of His love.

It is at His leading that I openly share this testimony. It is my prayer that it will give you the courage to seek refuge in the arms of our loving Father. He is waiting for you.

◆　◆　◆

A Word to Dear Pro-Life Warriors

When I talk to people about my involvement with Crisis Pregnancy Ministry, some will innocently rattle off a pro-life bumper sticker slogan like, "Great 'choice'…baby killing!" I know they are attempting to affirm my involvement with this ministry and show me that they understand what it's all about. Unfortunately, they don't know I'm a post-abortive Christian and their comments bring blows to wounds still tender and condemnation for sins forgiven.

God wants to heal the broken post-abortive hearts that are hiding behind the false security of secrecy. We must not trap these precious hurting souls in their painful prisons by standing in the way of God's plan of forgiveness and redemption. Even well-intentioned pro-lifers can create an atmosphere of judgment and condemnation. Until this ends, the voices that can most intimately tell about the devastation from abortion will remain silent.

Therefore, we should guard our lips as we share our hearts about abortion to ensure that our words express love, Grace, and mercy. We must be just as concerned about not building a judgmental wall between a post-abortive woman and God's Grace as we are about protecting the life of the unborn. God loves both equally—women and their unborn.

Post-abortive women can personally and powerfully attest to the lies shrouded in the pro-choice message. If we want to put an end to abortion, we must help these women to access Grace and to receive their healing so they can shout their stories! Then I think we will make great strides in defeating the enemy and the damage caused by abortion.

—Lisa Nolan

Editor's note: The ABC Women's Center in Middletown, Connecticut, where Lisa found support can be contacted through their website at www.ABCWomensCenter.org.

Chapter Eleven

My Pregnancy Would Have Embarrassed My Family

My beloved husband, Bruce, has helped me find peace with God, myself, and my two aborted children. As a memorial to them, he lovingly built a children's garden in our backyard. I was moved to tears by this compassionate undertaking. Among the flowering plants and next to the birdbath, he placed a beautiful stone sculpture of two children sitting together on a bench. This delightful garden has been such a blessing.

◆ ◆ ◆

On my journey to find healing from my abortions, I was privileged to attend a Rachel's Vineyard Retreat. One night we had a candlelight service where we gave names to our aborted babies. I prayed and asked God to help me name my children. The first name that came to mind was Sarah. Then I had a picture in my mind of a guardian, and the name "Michael" popped into my head. Quietly, I lit a candle for each of them and placed them afloat with other candles in a large crystal bowl. The little twinkling lights circling on the water was a lovely yet heart-wrenching sight.

After that, we were asked to relax as background music played softly and to let our minds take us to a beautiful meadow. In my mind I saw children—happy children of all ages and ethnic backgrounds—laughing and playing. It was such a joyful scene. Then to my right I saw a man with a gentle smile and such kind eyes. He had two beautiful children in his arms. As he walked toward me, I felt warmth and love. The children were so excited. He let the little boy, who was about four, stand up, and he placed the two-year-old girl in my arms. They smelled so sweet and their smiles were filled with love and joy.

At that moment I realized who was standing in front of me, and my heart exploded with gratitude! Jesus had brought my children to me...Sarah and Michael. They were all giggles and smiles. They gave me a lovely bouquet of flowers...smelling of forgiveness. They had forgiven me years ago. Now it was my turn to forgive myself.

Too soon, the time in the meadow was ending, and I stayed there watching Jesus lead my children and the others—joyfully running and jumping and skipping—back to heaven. Even today, this comforting scene is as real to me as watching my grandchildren playing in our backyard.

When I returned from the retreat and told my husband that I had named my children, he asked me if he could give them his last name. I was overwhelmed, and I wept. In writing this, I still weep as I consider Bruce's loving gesture of spiritually adopting Sarah and Michael.

◆　◆　◆

But let me back up to a time when I was twenty years old and pregnant. I wasn't sure who the father was; I had been dating and sleeping with two different men. One man was honorable; he wanted to marry me and give his child life. The other man refused to acknowledge that he might be the father. There was another complication. My dad was trying to become a deacon in our church, and it would never do if it was known that his unmarried daughter was pregnant.

I decided to have the baby and raise it on my own. When I told my mother, she exploded. "How could you do that to our family? What will our church friends think? What about the effect of this on your brothers?" Later, she continued her scolding. "You're selfish and spoiled to even think of having this baby, much less keeping it."

I became very afraid when I realized that my mother was not willing to help me parent my baby. I felt compelled, forced, and coerced…and cowardly, for not saying, "No, this is my child, and this is my body." It was as though I was frozen, as she made the appointment for the abortion.

Because my pregnancy was so far along, my abortion procedure took two days. The money had to be paid up front. My mother drove me to the clinic in Eugene, Oregon, on a cold, blustery day in February. They stuffed laminaria, a dried seaweed, into my cervix and sent me home. They gave me two Valium pills. I took one that night and one the next morning before my mother drove me back to the clinic.

I don't remember too much, other than I was scared. I asked if I could change my mind and the doctor explained, "Since we've already inserted the laminaria, the fetus is dead. We're going to do something similar to a D and C…no problem, don't worry." I believed that the fetus was dead and wouldn't feel a thing.

On a table next to where I lay, they covered two large glass jars with a small cloth and began the suctioning. The cover slipped off the jars, and I saw the color red. That's all I remember until I was walking out and was told to go out a different door than the one I came in. I felt numb.

Afterward, my mom took me to a restaurant. I wasn't hungry. I wasn't angry. I didn't cry. I just sat there and listened to my mom say, "It's for the best, honey; now you can get on with your life."

During the next three years, I denied the abortion, tried to forget it, and tried to get up every morning like it mattered. When I attempted to talk to my mother about the abortion, she would say, "Honey, you just have to forget about it. Don't be so melodramatic! Grow up; life goes on."

Melodramatic, a word I heard often. I hated that word. It belittled my feelings, as though they didn't matter.

Three years after my abortion, I met a kind, good-looking man and soon I moved into his apartment. Glenn was thirty-six; I was twenty-three. He was going through a tough divorce, and I knew I could help him, and he was just what I needed. He had two children of his own, and he was helping to raise his ex-wife's two children. When his divorce was final, we planned to marry and have one child of our own. It seemed ideal. There I was...not married, not attending church, drinking, and smoking marijuana. But I was certain this man loved me.

He lied. When the divorce was final, he decided that he wasn't ready to get married. Then he decided he didn't want more children, so he had a vasectomy. At the time, we didn't know I was already pregnant.

The next month when I confirmed my pregnancy, he was furious. He gave me an ultimatum. I could have this child and be on my own with no help from him. Or I could have an abortion and help him raise his children as my own. "They are already here," he said, "and they need both of us."

I couldn't believe it. Early on when I had told him about my abortion, he was sympathetic and wanted to give me a child. Now he was totally different. He didn't want another child, and he made my choice perfectly clear. It was him or the baby; his living children or the baby. I fought him; I begged and I cried. To no avail. My mother agreed that abortion was an option and was okay.

I made the abortion appointment and Glenn drove me. He waited outside as I went into the doctor's office alone. When I came out, he didn't even ask me how I was.

This was our weekend to have his kids, Jack and Sadie, and so from the abortion clinic we drove 150 miles to pick up the children, then turned around and drove 150 miles home. That weekend I cooked and cleaned and cared for his children...all the while dying inside. There was no time for weeping; no one to talk to. I wanted to die, but I was too scared to take my own life. I kept picturing how the children would feel if I committed suicide. I couldn't do that to them. I was already packing enough guilt for all of us.

Glenn and I never spoke of that abortion...ever. He never once asked how I was or if I was okay. I didn't go for the follow-up appointment with the doctor. I shoved all the feelings and pain as far away as I could. I started smoking marijuana daily and continued the drug use for ten years.

Finally, I decided it was time to quit using marijuana as a crutch and after years of living a life of drugs, I was clean. Then it was time to get a good job and I did just that. Unfortunately I had an affair with my boss, Tony, who was married, and I left Glenn for two months. He called and begged me to come home, so I did. I missed his children, Jack and Sadie. Two years later, I took another job with a different company, only I ended up with the same boss. Once again Tony made me feel special, so we resumed our relationship after I left Glenn permanently. The hardest part about leaving was telling Glenn's children. They were angry at me for leaving their dad, and I haven't heard from them in the fourteen years since then. I ended the relationship with Tony after five months, when I finally realized how painful it was for me and for Tony's wife.

I still hadn't talked with anyone about my abortions. I didn't think about them anymore, but I avoided pregnant women whenever possible.

A few months later, on April 1, I called Bruce Marcy. He worked as a disabled veterans specialist in the state employment office, and I knew him because of my job at a lumber mill. I hung up the telephone four times before I finally mustered up courage to talk to him. I explained that a friend had given me two tickets to a charity ball, and I invited him to go with me. He thought it was a joke since it was April Fool's Day. I told him it wasn't a joke. He accepted my invitation and six months later we were married.

Bruce had been married before and had two lovely daughters, Nancy, twenty-three, and Lesa, eighteen. Lesa gave birth to a son, and I became an instant grandma! What a joy!

Bruce had previously had a vasectomy and since we both wanted children, we began looking into having his vasectomy reversed. We found out that it was an expensive surgery, and so we decided to purchase a home first and then save up the money required for the reversal.

One night I was awakened by a funny feeling. I threw back the covers and stood up. I realized there was blood all over me and the bedding and some of it was on Bruce. I was hemorrhaging! My immediate thought was to clean everything up before Bruce woke up and got upset. He is a decorated Vietnam combat veteran with a severe case of post-traumatic stress disorder.

While I was in the bathroom cleaning myself up, Bruce sleepily stumbled in and asked what was wrong. I told him that I was okay, but I was bleeding a little more than normal. When he discovered the amount of blood on the bed, he insisted we contact the doctor.

The next morning during our consultation I told the doctor about my two abortions. He examined me and did a vaginal ultrasound. He said I was bleeding internally, and he believed it was due to a perforated uterus which resulted from an injury that occurred during my second abortion and endometriosis had set in. The doctor said my uterus, ovaries, and bladder were all involved; they looked like one big black blob on the ultrasound screen. He said, "You have no choice, you must have a hysterectomy."

My dreams of motherhood ended that day in the doctor's office. I didn't have any choice in this matter...I had used up my choices.

This is when I realized I needed more in my life, and I began my journey to God. One Sunday, a friend asked me to attend church with her, and I said, "Sure, why not?" We went to her Catholic church and I witnessed the True Presence of Christ. I continued to go to her church, and I was overjoyed and filled with awe. Not only did Jesus Christ die on the cross for me, I felt His presence at every Mass!

My husband and I are like the prodigal son talked about in the Bible, and thanks be to God, both of us were welcomed with open arms to a True Feast and to rejoicing, the likes of which I had never experienced. We were not raised Catholic. As a matter of fact, my husband was raised in the Mormon religion and I attended church irregularly as a child.

We wanted all we could get of this new relationship with God, so we planned to attend the weekly sessions of the Rite of Christian Initiation of Adults. But before I could begin these classes, I knew that I had to speak with Father Terry. I had to know if God, and the Church, would welcome someone who had killed her own children. That walk to the rectory for my appointment was the longest walk I have ever made. When I asked if I could join the Catholic Church, I could only tell him about the first abortion. I chickened out and could not bring myself to admit that I had aborted two children. Once again, I was a coward. But God knew and made my confession whole, even though I wasn't able to tell the whole story.

Father Terry was saddened because I thought I wasn't worthy to be a child of God. Reconciliation was my first step in a long journey to healing, and thanks be to God, I took that first step under the guidance of this understanding priest.

My husband and I have traveled together on this road to peace with God, and the journey has been one of the most joy-filled times in my life.

◆　◆　◆

Before my mother died of brain cancer, she asked me to forgive her for pushing me into that first abortion I hadn't wanted. She said she knew how that decision had led me to make a second bad "choice." My mother died knowing that I had forgiven her. She also forgave me for my anger toward her. I know that our Heavenly Father loved my mother and also forgave her...long before she knew to ask. She is united with her grandchildren in heaven, and they are waiting for my arrival, when we will rejoice together.

◆　◆　◆

When one of my daughters, by marriage, was pregnant with our twin granddaughters, she invited me to her doctor's appointments where I actually heard the girls' heartbeats and saw them moving on ultrasound. Both of "our" daughters asked me to be present when they gave birth. I don't know which was better— seeing and hearing these grandbabies in the womb or holding them at birth. But in both, I witnessed Grace.

◆　◆　◆

Many friends came to our home for a barbeque and to witness the blessing by Father Karl of the children's garden that Bruce had so lovingly built, not only as a memorial to my children but also for all the victims of abortion…and for their mothers. Father Karl offered the most consoling prayer for Sarah and Michael and for the other children of abortion. Then he prayed for the mothers who had lost their children.

It has been thirty years since my first abortion, and there hasn't been a day that I haven't thought about my children, Sarah and Michael. It is in their memory and for them that I prayerfully offer "our" story of love and forgiveness. Being able to tell this story has been a long time in coming. Because of the healing that came from God, now I can remember my children with love, not shame.

My prayer is that those who read my story will understand that it isn't just the babies that are killed by abortion, but a part of every woman dies who has chosen this path. A pregnant woman should *not* be forced to choose between the conflicting wants and needs of herself and those around her, and the life of her children. A woman's rights should and must include the right to bear children in a safe, loving, and welcoming environment.

There is hope! Hope in the Name of God.

—Suzan Marcy

Editor's note: Suzan found help and support at a Rachel's Vineyard Retreat, an organization listed in the Appendix. Their website is www.RachelsVineyard.org and their telephone number is 1-877-HOPE 4 ME.

Chapter Twelve

My Doctor Said, "Your Life Could Be In Danger!"

I grew up in a small town in Arkansas and was honored as one of the top ten at my high school graduation. I have always been outgoing with many good friends. I met and married Dail, a wonderful Christian man, finished college, became a middle school science teacher, and we had a beautiful son.

At age twenty-six, my doctor discovered a tumor on my bladder. Our whole church prayed for me, and I believed it was an answer to prayer when I was admitted into a program to try an experimental drug that held great promise as a cure for intercystital cystosis.

Soon after I started this medicine, I became pregnant. Dail and I and our whole family were excited, especially three-year-old Jonathan. But my doctor wasn't happy. Because of the medication, he told me I could not have this baby because my life could be in danger and that my baby could be a monster. He said, "You must decide quickly to have a D and C before the heart starts beating." He never talked to me about alternatives.

I was seven weeks pregnant, and at the time, I did not know a baby's heart is beating just three weeks after conception. Looking back, I don't know why the doctor gave me the wrong information or why he would not use the word "abortion" to describe what he wanted me to do.

I was overwhelmed by the doctor's words and very scared. I left his office crying and immediately called my husband to ask him what we should do. We called our parents and other close family members and they prayed with us. I honestly thought I had to get this "cleaning out" so I wouldn't die. The thought of not being there to raise Jonathan added to the pressure. Also, I thought I would never forgive myself for delivering "a monster." My husband's encouragement to end the pregnancy was primarily motivated by his concern for me. We decided to heed the doctor's advice. I thought I had no other choice.

My doctor sent me to a Planned Parenthood facility in Little Rock. I wondered why my doctor didn't do the procedure and care for me himself since this was an at-risk pregnancy.

As my husband drove into the clinic parking lot, people on the sidewalk solemnly held up signs that read "Save your baby." I huddled down in the seat and said, "Oh, honey, they don't know why we are here, do they?" I still thought this was just tissue that had to come out of me.

Surely this wasn't a baby, I thought; *the doctor said the heart wasn't beating.*

Inside, I signed in and paid the fee. No counselors spoke to me and soon I was ushered into a cold, stark room with bare walls. I was lying on a table that was so cold I shivered. A nurse told me it would be over quickly and I could return to work the next day. She said it wouldn't hurt.

She was absolutely wrong!

A man came in. I presumed he was a doctor. He didn't say anything. As soon as I heard the suction machine, I began to wonder, "What's happening to me?"

After the procedure was over, I was taken to another room and told to sit for a while. Several younger girls were sitting in chairs lined up against the wall. A girl, who looked like she was about sixteen, asked, "Was yours a boy or a girl?" I was shocked! *What did she mean? Surely, this wasn't a baby! Not yet!*

On the way home, I was in excruciating pain. At home standing in my kitchen, I began hemorrhaging. Dail helped me to the bathroom where I passed more bloody pieces! After I got into bed, I called my mother, but she said that maybe we shouldn't talk about it. I felt too ashamed to call the doctor. Although the doctor called it a D and C, I knew Planned Parenthood did abortions.

Oh, God. What did I do? I cried myself to sleep that night.

Because I was having such a terrible time dealing with my loss, my doctor suggested that I get pregnant right away—as though this would replace the child I lost and fill the empty void. So after I finished the medication for my tumor, I got pregnant again. During this pregnancy, I asked God to punish me by giving me a deformed child or by taking my life. I am now thankful that God didn't give me what I asked, but instead blessed me with Jared, a normal, healthy baby born one year after my abortion.

I was overly protective of Jared and Jonathan. I was fearful of injury or death, afraid that harm would come to them as my punishment. I wouldn't let them out of my sight.

For twelve years, I tried to push this experience out of my mind talking only to my husband about it, not admitting the truth to myself of what I had done. Many nights I cried myself to sleep in his arms although I still justified my abortion as different because I *had* to do it.

My husband and I both believe our child was a girl, and we named her Jill Allison. I often dreamed about my little girl, but I couldn't talk about her to others. We wouldn't get to celebrate her first birthday or her first day of school, or wouldn't push her in a swing or see her smile. I know some might say, "If you had died or your baby was 'a monster,' you could not have enjoyed those events." That could be. But because I chose abortion, I will never know. I do know that my baby's size, the level of her physical and mental development, and her possible dependency and special needs did not justify her death.

I became addicted to work and had low self-esteem and repressed anger. I had difficulty making decisions and being close to friends, and I was unable to relax. I had many pelvic infections and endometriosis, and eventually had to have a hysterectomy.

During this long, desperate time, if it had it not been for my relationship with God, I think I would have lost my mind. At times, I'm sure my husband thought I had lost my mind. When the abortion clinic nurse told me, "This will be over quickly," she didn't tell me that I would regret it for the rest of my life.

Even though my situation might be viewed as a "tough case" and one that many people would consider a justifiable reason for abortion, I still consider it a tragic and irreversible choice that has caused me deep pain and regret.

Finally, I took positive steps to begin the healing process.

I learned that grieving, which is so important in healing, is quashed by a society that doesn't want to hear and doesn't understand. My guilt and shame also caused me to keep my secret hidden. Until women identify their need to grieve their loss and are encouraged to do so; they will continue to experience emotional and psychological trauma.

◆　◆　◆

I went back to school and received a master's degree in counseling education. After being in private practice for a time, I became director of Concepts of Truth, Inc., a nonprofit counseling and pregnancy care center. In that role, I coordinate and answer telephone calls for a national helpline for abortion recovery. I have talked with many women who deeply regret their abortions. These women, who have lived with post-abortion trauma, find relief as they work through the healing process.

This sampling of comments, from the telephone calls that I have received, illustrates the devastating trauma that abortion piles on women:

> *Although her abortion had been several years before, one caller stated, "My guilt won't go away."*

> *A teenager said, "My girlfriend had an abortion about a week ago and is acting strange. She won't talk to me about it."*

> *One mother said, "I see how painful it is for my daughter, so I want to help others not make this mistake."*

> *A 66-year-old lady who had three abortions said, "I want to talk and get it right."*

> *Another caller said, "I've never talked about my abortion that happened twenty-eight years ago." She said, "I didn't know it was an abortion center. No one counseled me. The doctor told me there was no heartbeat. My husband tells me, 'Forget it.'"*

> *One caller said she has attempted suicide three times and has mutilated herself by cutting her body with a razor blade. She is tormented by thoughts of what she did to her child. At the abortion clinic she was not given counseling and was told to be quiet during the painful procedure.*

> *A woman who had five abortions has been under psychiatric care for five years but said her counselor cannot understand her pain.*

> *Another said, "I don't know how to forgive myself, but I would do anything if I could just help one other person avoid what I'm going through. This is just awful."*

One caller felt that her abortion twenty-five years before had ruined her life. She said she went downhill and had a second abortion and lost all self-esteem. She has actually lived in cars and has panic attacks. At the time of her call, she was contemplating suicide.

Another caller has difficulty in relationships since her abortion. She has been married six times.

Another caller suffers with depression. Her present husband doesn't know about her abortion, and she has not been able to conceive.

A woman developed a serious case of dermatitis shortly after her abortion. It was so serious—with severe rashes and oozing sores—she avoided being around other people. Doctors could not find a medical cause for her condition. After she got pregnant again, the condition cleared up. After looking into it, she believes the dermatitis was a result of stress after her abortion. She has researched the possible link of women having autoimmune diseases because of the trauma of abortion.

Another caller had one abortion and five miscarriages. She was upset because she felt pressured by the baby's father. He didn't want the baby.

A caller stated she was an alcoholic and addicted to drugs. She believes these addictions were related to her abortion that happened eleven years before.

A caller who had just had an abortion ten days before was very upset. Her parents and doctor advised her to abort because she was just twenty years old. She said she felt very sad and was having nightmares.

◆ ◆ ◆

Abortion is the irreversible choice that hurt me and took the life of my daughter. Going through a Bible study for abortion recovery and giving Jill Allison her personhood and identity have been important parts of my grieving and healing. For years, shame caused me to be silent. No more! I give her purpose and honor today by sharing my story with you.

—Millie Lace, MSE, LPC

Editor's note: Millie is a licensed professional counselor in Arkansas. She is director of Concepts of Truth, Inc., and coordinates the National Helpline for Abortion Recovery, which can be reached at 1-866-482-LIFE. She is also the state leader for Operation Outcry: Silent No More.

Her husband, Dail, works with post-abortive men.

Chapter Thirteen

My Husband Insisted On the Abortion

I submitted to an abortion. I wasn't young or inexperienced. I was forty-two, married, and the mother of two boys, ages nine and three.

Years before, my insurance company terminated my maternity coverage. To reinstate it would have cost $150 a month, which I couldn't afford. Then a few months before I got pregnant, I failed to pay my health insurance premium and the coverage terminated. So I had no medical insurance and a history of pre-term labor and a previous pregnancy that cost more than $100,000.

My husband, Ralph, urged me to consider an abortion. "We're too old," he said. He insisted that our comfort and the comfort of our two boys, Danny and Alex, were threatened. "After all," he said, "I'm not asking you to do anything illegal."

We argued about it for days. He knew I wanted this baby, and he said he would support me either way. But, he said, if I had this child we would have no more vacations, no more eating out, and no more money toward college for our kids. Also, I could no longer pay for the plane tickets for my mother to come visit us. He said I would have to give him all the money I earned. And he didn't even know that my medical insurance policy had been canceled.

I cried and told him over and over that I knew that I could not live with my conscience if I did what he wanted me to do.

I finally gave in. I was a coward, my faith was weak, and I was afraid to take the full responsibility in case something went wrong. I worried. I knew that, because of my age, there was a higher likelihood of having a baby with Down syndrome. What then?

I went to the abortion clinic with the idea of stopping the procedure at the last minute. That way, I thought, I could appease my husband. At least it would seem like I had tried to please him. Looking back, I realize I was afraid of my husband.

When we got to the clinic, the woman at the front desk asked me what kind of abortion I wanted. *None*, I thought to myself. Ralph immediately jumped in and said, "She has not made up her mind yet. Is there any counselor she can talk to?" We were led into a counseling room by a woman with a pleasant smile. After we sat down, I told her, "Deep inside my heart I know there is no justification for an abortion."

Ralph glared at me. He said, "She thinks she's carrying a baby and not just a blob of cells." The counselor assured me that my baby was "just a pinhead." Both she and my husband argued with me. She said, "You can do this. You don't have to want it or like it. It's best to make this sacrifice for the well-being of your two boys." My husband begged me, "Please do it!"

How naive and stupid I was. I did not even object when the counselor compared my baby to a tumor. "Wouldn't you remove a tumor?" she said. As she shoved the papers at me to sign, she told me, "You can stop the abortion at any time."

When it was time to go into the operating room, I crouched down outside the door and whimpered, "I can't do this." Two smiling women, one on each side of me, lifted me up and pushed me into the room. The doctor was upset with me because I was crying. Many times, I told him, "I don't want to. I don't want to!" They gave me the anesthesia, and I went to sleep praying, actually yelling, "Our Father who art in heaven...." I don't know if I was asking God to save my baby or to forgive me for killing him.

When I woke up, I felt violated and hurt. I thought to myself, *I'm not pregnant anymore.* Immediately I realized my baby was gone forever! I had committed the most terrible crime of my life!

In that moment of realization, my living hell started. I felt my life was ruined, and I thought of suicide so I could join my baby in the afterlife. On the way home from the clinic, I thought about throwing myself out of the car on the expressway. *But what if I don't die immediately? If Ralph has to take me to the hospital, he will find out that I didn't pay the insurance premium and that I have no medical insurance.* I was afraid to do it.

That night when my crying kept Ralph awake, he yelled at me, "What's wrong with you? We got rid of the problem!" The next morning, after a night without sleep, I urged Ralph to look on the Internet for what happened to women after an abortion.

He searched WebMD and found only one article. He showed it to me and pointed to one sentence: "Most women do not regret abortion." He grinned knowingly and said, "You see? You're crazy, you're creating this problem. You'll be okay." I cried.

Later he found a website about post-abortion depression. After he read the information, he looked sad. He hugged me, and for the first time in the ten years of our marriage he apologized. He said, "I'm sorry. Forgive me." Even though it took the website information to open his eyes and soften his heart, I felt that somehow he understood and shared my pain.

He found a psychologist who saw me that afternoon, and Ralph told her he was willing do everything in his power to help me. The psychologist referred me to a psychiatrist and two days later I was able to see him. He prescribed antidepressant medication for me.

My husband had urged me to abort my baby for the wellbeing of our other two children, Danny and Alex. But after the abortion, I found myself incapable of taking care of them for almost a year. I held my two innocent boys responsible for the death of their sibling. This seems irrational and insane, but at the time I couldn't help myself. Why could they breathe, talk, and laugh, and my baby couldn't? Why were their future and their comfort and their college money more important than my third child's life? I stopped talking to them. I could not hug them. Their presence bothered me.

What kind of a monster was I? I had killed my third child and was unable to love my first and second.

Before the abortion, my husband liked to sleep late and go play tennis after work. Even though I had a job, he left the responsibility for the children entirely up to me. I took care of them before and after school, and helped them with their homework.

After the abortion, my husband's life changed drastically. He had to take over and care for our kids. He found himself doing what he had neglected for so many years—in addition to now having to take care of me.

My days were filled with anger, depression, anxiety, and flashbacks of the abortion. I remember wanting capital punishment. I was determined to get myself arrested so I could confess to this murder. I knew this plan wouldn't work, so my thoughts turned to suicide. I tried to hang myself but was too cowardly to finish. I thought of driving into a canal. I was intentionally very close to being hit by a truck. I would go walking in the middle of the night, hoping I would get lost or die. I cut myself and hit myself many times. I refused to eat. I went to work, but even there I cried most of the time. The rest of the time I spent in bed hoping to die. I was helpless to do anything about my miserable life. The therapy and medication didn't seem to help. There was no magic therapy or pill to cure my sorrow, grief, regrets, anger, and anguish.

My family and friends were concerned about my personality change, but I didn't dare tell them about the abortion. I just said I was sick and being treated for depression.

I had turned my anger inward, blaming myself. I had failed to protect the most amazing gift that God had given me. Deep inside I knew that regardless of the outside pressure, I was responsible for that life, and I could not forgive myself for this crime. My husband and my psychologist urged me not to direct all my anger at myself.

My husband acknowledged his guilt, and I started to hate him. I was so angry at him; I hit him on several occasions. I blamed him for being so cruel to me the night of the abortion. I reminded him over and over that, "It was your magnificent idea to kill our child! You promised me that our lives would be unchanged!" I blamed him for convincing me that I had to sacrifice my child for the well-being of my family, that it was not important what I wanted, what I believed, but that it was my duty to have the abortion. I blamed him for not defending me at the clinic and for taking sides against me with the abortion counselor. I blamed him because I had to endure all the pain, depression, regrets, and hopelessness after the abortion. I blamed him for ruining my life!

About a month after the abortion, he started to write about his feelings, but he made the mistake of showing me what he had written. I was furious at him and hurt to read that he considered it my fault for refusing his demands to have a tubal ligation after our second child was born. I understood this to mean that he did not regret the abortion, only the fact that I had gotten pregnant for the third time.

I reacted horribly and was determined to leave. I did not want anything from this man who at the moment I could not love—or hate. I felt completely indifferent.

After my husband promised me we would have another child, I committed myself to concentrate on healing. Seven months after the abortion, I got pregnant again. I found out that I was pregnant on the exact due date of my aborted child, whom I had named Gabi. I was really happy and thanked God for such a sign of forgiveness.

Sadly, I miscarried very early. It was very painful, but not nearly as painful as the abortion.

I hadn't been able to tell people about Gabi and the abortion. But after the miscarriage, it was different. I was able to speak about this lost child whom I named Gabriela Melissa. Even though most people could not understand my pain, they were sympathetic. This allowed me to mourn both of my babies; although no one knew that I was mourning an aborted child as well. Talking about an abortion experience is much more difficult than sharing about a miscarriage.

Then two years after my miscarriage, I got pregnant again, but I miscarried Valeria Isabel at nine weeks. I now believe that my abortion did not kill just one child but three—Gabi, Mel, and Val. I have learned that injury to the cervix or scarring to the uterine wall during an abortion can cause miscarriages.

◆ ◆ ◆

From the beginning I somehow knew that God was my only hope. But how could I turn to him after what I had done? I was fortunate that I was referred to Father Gabriel, and he introduced me to the Merciful God I had forgotten. Thanks to God's mercy, many Bible studies, a Rachel's Vineyard Retreat, and many wonderful pro-life workers who God placed in my path, my healing journey began. It took a lot of Bible studies and prayers before I was able to forgive myself…and to forgive my husband.

I came to understand that God allowed His son, Jesus Christ, to die on the cross for the forgiveness of my sins. That included the horrible sin of my abortion. I was able to accept God's forgiveness and believe that my baby forgave me for extinguishing his light before he had the chance to shine. Then I was able to forgive the abortionist and the clinic personnel, leaving their judgment in God's hands.

It has not been an easy road. I realize that the healing and restoration after my abortion required a miracle. Our marriage was shaken many times, but thanks to God and His amazing grace it has survived. This tragedy gave both myself and my husband a tremendous lesson, and brought us closer to God, to each other, and to our living children, Danny and Alex. Only God, with His great love for us, could use something so hideous to strengthen our family. Only He is capable of such a miracle!

◆ ◆ ◆

Since I can't bring Gabi or my two miscarried babies back, I pledge to honor them by speaking the truth about the horrors of abortion. Abortion does not erase a pregnancy. It kills a child and scars a woman for life! No one can hurt a baby without hurting his or her mother. I have suffered greatly—physically, emotionally and spiritually. My children and my husband also have had to pay the consequences.

Abortion does not help women; it hurts women!

I am determined to do what I can and I hope that others who have been hurt by abortion will speak up. I think that if my husband and I had heard or read such a testimony, Gabi would be alive! I pray that my story will help save the lives of unborn children by turning their parents away from abortion and that mothers, fathers, and siblings will be spared the terrible aftermath of abortion.

I did not know who to turn to for support when my husband was pressuring me to have the abortion. I didn't know that crisis pregnancy centers existed to help women. I wish these centers were located next to abortion clinics and that information about their ministries was more widely advertised.

◆ ◆ ◆

I still mourn for my babies every day, and probably will continue to do so until I see them in heaven. I am the mother of a child destroyed by abortion and two children lost through miscarriage; nothing will change these sad parts of my life's story. But being able to share my story has been an important part of my healing journey. Thank you for giving me this opportunity to tell you about God's love.

—Luz Marina Tamayo

Editor's note: Luz found help and support at a Rachel's Vineyard Retreat, an organization listed in the Appendix. Their website is www.RachelsVineyard.org and their telephone number is 1-877-HOPE 4 ME.

Luz is also involved with the Silent No More Awareness Campaign. Their website is www.SilentNoMoreAwareness.org.

Chapter Fourteen

I Was Threatened

I have a rich family heritage of courageous Christian folks whose activities have made a difference in the world. My father, Reverend A. D. King, was a preacher and civil rights activist. My grandfather was Martin Luther King, Sr. My uncle was Martin Luther King, Jr. My Dad and his brother, my Uncle Martin, were often referred to as "sons of thunder," because of their preaching styles.

But our family reflects tragedy as well as triumph. I was a teenager when my father died. My grandmother was shot and killed as she played the organ in church. Uncle Martin was shot and killed in Memphis, Tennessee. My home in Birmingham, Alabama, was bombed.

◆ ◆ ◆

I grew up in the South during the turbulent times of the fifties and sixties. I am a mother of six living children, and I am a grandmother. I am also a post-abortive mother.

In the early 1970s, I suffered one involuntary and one voluntary abortion. My involuntary abortion was performed by my private physician—without my consent! I had gone to the doctor to ask why my cycle had not resumed after the birth of my son. I did not ask for and did not want an abortion.

The doctor said, "You don't need to be pregnant, let's see." He performed a painful examination which resulted in a gush

94

of blood and tissue. He explained, "I performed a local D and C."

Soon after the *Roe v. Wade* Supreme Court decision in 1973, I became pregnant again. The baby's father pressured me to have an abortion and threatened physical violence. The ease and convenience provided through *Roe v. Wade* made it too easy for me to make the fateful and fatal decision to abort our child. I went to a doctor and he said, "The procedure won't hurt any more than having a tooth pulled." The next day, I was admitted to the hospital, and our baby was aborted. My medical insurance paid for the procedure.

As soon as I woke up, I knew something was terribly wrong. I felt very ill—and very empty. I tried to talk to the doctor and nurses about it, but they didn't want to listen. They simply assured me that "it will all go away in a few days. You will be fine." They were wrong.

I felt angry about both abortions, and guilty about the abortion I chose to have. The guilt made me dreadfully ill. I began to suffer from eating disorders, depression, nightmares, sexual dysfunctions, and a host of other serious problems.

Over the next few years, I had trouble bonding with my son and his five siblings who were born after the abortions. My children have all suffered from knowing that they have a brother or sister that their mother chose to abort. Often they ask if I ever thought about aborting them. They have even said to me, "You killed our baby." This is extremely painful for all of us.

Also, my mother and my grandparents were saddened to know about the loss of the baby. The aborted child's father now regrets the abortion. If it had not been for *Roe v. Wade*, I would never have had that abortion.

With my testimony, I join the voices of thousands of post-abortive women across America, who will no longer be silent. I cannot sit idly by as this horrible spirit of murder cuts down our unborn, and destroys the lives of post-abortive mothers. For me, and countless abortive mothers, nothing on earth can fully restore what has been lost. Our arms will always feel empty.

◆　◆　◆

I was born on January 22, and each year my birthday is marred by the fact that this date is also the anniversary of *Roe v. Wade*, the Supreme Court decision that has spelled death for millions of babies. My deceased children and I are victims of abortion; the *Roe v. Wade* decision has adversely affected the lives of my entire family.

We march to cure breast cancer, yet many promote abortion, which is one of the biggest causes. Studies show there are direct links between abortion and serious conditions such as breast and cervical cancer, emotional disorders, and other ills! I've experienced the emotional disorders, and I still worry about these other threats of cervical and breast cancer.

◆　◆　◆

In the ongoing abortion debate, a voice in the wilderness continues to cry out, "What about the children?" We have been fueled by the fire of "women's rights" for so long we have become deaf to the outcry of the victims whose rights are being trampled upon—the babies and the mothers. We cannot continue to ignore the cry for mercy from the unborn and the suffering of the mothers.

A woman does have the right to decide what to do with her own body. Thank God for the U.S. Constitution. But what about the rights of each female baby who is aborted? Partial birth abortion is perhaps the most heinous form of this legal genocide. What about the rights of that unborn woman who is artificially breached before coming to term, then has her skull punctured, and who agonizingly suffers as the life drains out of her? God had wonderful plans for each of these unborn women—plans to pioneer exciting frontiers in this new millennium. What about the rights of these millions of unborn women?

Uncle Martin, in his "I Have A Dream" speech in 1963, said: "I have a dream...that my four little children will one day live in a nation where they will not be judged by the color of their skin but by the content of their character."

It would have broken his heart if he had lived to see the contents of thousands of children's skulls emptied into the bottomless caverns of the abortionists' pits.

In that same speech, MLK said: "Five score years ago, Abraham Lincoln signed the Emancipation Proclamation. This decree came as a joyous daybreak to end the long night of Negro slavery."

I say we still have slavery in this country. Every unborn baby is like property, a slave in the womb of his or her mother. This slavery will continue as long as a mother is allowed to legally decide her baby's fate—whether her child will live...or die.

If the "dream" of MLK is to live, our babies must live. Our mothers must choose life.

My uncle said: "When the architects of our republic wrote the magnificent words of the Constitution and the Declaration of Independence, they were signing a promissory note to which every American was to fall heir. This note was a promise that all men, yes, black men as well as white men, would be guaranteed the inalienable rights of life, liberty, and the pursuit of happiness."

◆　◆　◆

I, too, dream.

I have a dream of a time when this magnificent promise of the inalienable rights of life, liberty, and the pursuit of happiness will again extend to the weakest and most helpless of our nation—our unborn citizens.

I have a dream that we will come to our senses, and humble ourselves before God Almighty, pray for mercy, and receive His healing grace. He promises: "If my people, who are called by my name, will humble themselves and pray and seek my face and turn from their wicked ways, then will I hear from heaven and will forgive their sin and will heal their land." (2 Chronicles 7:14)

It is time for America, perhaps the most blessed nation on earth, to lead the world in repentance, and in restoration of *life*.

I have a dream that we will again recognize that life is sacred, is God-given, and is something to celebrate.

I have a dream that this is the day, the hour of our deliverance. I pray that a Spirit of Repentance will sweep our land. I pray that God will have mercy on us all.

—Dr. Alveda King

Editor's note: Dr. Alveda King is a civil rights activist, a minister of the Gospel of Jesus Christ, a former college professor, and an author. She has served in the Georgia State House of Representatives for four years and is an accomplished actress and songwriter. Alveda received her honorary doctorate of laws from Saint Anslem College.

Chapter Fifteen

The First Time, I Chose Abortion— The Second Time, Adoption

At sixteen, I was confused. I thought that I had to be perfect. I was the classic overachiever, completely unaware that God knew that I wasn't perfect and He had never intended me to work so hard for His love. In the household I grew up in, love, respect, and trust were earned; even at a young age. My mother taught me, "Do whatever you have to do to get things done."

One day I felt faint and my mother took me to the hospital emergency room. I thought I might be pregnant, but the doctor said I was dehydrated. Later I went to our family physician who confirmed that I was pregnant. She said, "Do you want to tell your mother?"

"I'm afraid of what she will say."

"You could have an abortion," she said. She gave me a pamphlet and called an abortion clinic to make an appointment for me.

After being medicated for three years for bipolar disorder, I was a frantic teenager looking for the easiest way out of my unwanted pregnancy. I confronted my boyfriend with the idea of an abortion; he was not interested. I insisted; he gave in and agreed to pay part of the cost. He wasn't ready to be a father at eighteen.

Because I was only sixteen, the abortion clinic said they needed to notify my mother. When I told them I was afraid, they gave me the number of an attorney that could help me. They explained that a judge could give me a "judicial bypass" so I could have the abortion without my Mom knowing.

I made an appointment with the lawyer, and Larry drove me to a rundown area of town. I thought we were going to his office, but the address we were given was his home. We sat with him in a living room with lousy carpet and beat-up furniture. There was no air conditioning and it was very hot. It was weird.

He said I should tell the truth and asked, "Are your parents abusive?"

I didn't tell him everything, but I reluctantly explained how my mother had abused me physically and mentally. My earliest recollection was at age five when she hit me because I left some crayons in the car, and they melted and made a mess on the seat.

He advised me, "Tell the judge you're afraid of your mother and that you have plans after high school." Then he told me, "Don't say you're on medication for depression." Evidently in our state that fact would mean my mother *would* have to be notified. I felt like the plan was to manipulate the judge.

On Friday, we went before the judge. He asked me what plans I had after I finished high school. I said the first thing that came to mind: "Go to the Naval Academy." In fact, I had thought about joining the Navy.

The judge granted the judicial bypass, and the next day I walked into a "women's clinic" and had an abortion. Never have I felt such pain and guilt.

A month later, I stopped taking my medication and my bulimia spun out of control. I binged and purged many times every day. I even began cutting myself on my abdomen. I was hurting, big time, and the people who were supposed to care about me and love me, my family, didn't even notice I was suffering.

Then one day I was too weak to walk up the stairs and they became concerned. They took me to the hospital. I was depressed and cried continually. The nurses were worried about me. Of course, the doctor realized I had an eating disorder, told my mom and recommended I be transferred to a psychiatric hospital.

At the psych hospital I told a counselor about the abortion. I explained to her that was why my eating problem had gotten so crazy. She advised me to tell my mother about the abortion. But I didn't want to hurt my mother or grandmother.

One day while the counselor and my mother were in my room, I started crying. "What happened? Has anyone hurt you?" my mother demanded.

I told her, "Mom, I had an abortion."

At first she looked shocked, and then she cried and cried. The only other time I had seen her cry like that was when her sister was murdered. "Why?" she finally asked.

"I was afraid to tell you I was pregnant."

Then she got mad. She screamed at me. "You don't have to be afraid of me!"

After this, nothing mattered and my already shaky relationship with Mom got worse and every communication was confrontational. Daily, she reminded me how I had ruined her life and took her grandbaby away from her. I started doing drugs and my bulimia got worse.

A year later my boyfriend and I became pregnant again. I thought that by telling Mother, it would help us reconcile our poor relationship. But it didn't help.

Larry was very immature. He let me know he would rather continue smoking marijuana than raise a family with me.

I was ashamed and didn't want to live in my hometown, so I went to live at a maternity home for the remainder of my pregnancy. I didn't know that I would find God through the wonderful folks at Fatherheart Maternity Home in Lindale, Texas. Week after week I was taught about God's loving kindness, and His faithfulness, mercy, justice, and righteousness. The more I learned, the stronger my desire became to follow Him. I felt His loving arms comforting and strengthening me.

During my stay at Fatherheart, one of the staff guided me through a post-abortion healing Bible study. I learned that with the confession of my sins, the acknowledgement of Christ's death for me and the importance of the cross, that God's grace is sufficient for His children. I was able to admit my sin of murdering my child, who I named Malachi, and receive God's forgiveness.

For many months at Fatherheart I sought God's will for my life and the life of the precious daughter in my womb, who I had already named Adelia. One morning in our chapel worship service, I sensed the Holy Spirit asking me to trust Him with Adelia. I committed to put her future in God's hands. Soon after, the Holy Spirit spoke to my heart and impressed upon me that He wanted me to place Adelia with an adoptive family. I thought about that idea for several minutes and then said, "Yes."

Immediately I felt such peace. From that moment on, I pressed forward with an adoption plan knowing that it was God's will. And knowing that God wanted what was best for Adelia—and for me.

Opposition came quickly. No one in my family understood adoption. "How can you give your baby away?" each of them would argue. Trying to explain placement to a traditional Hispanic family was an impossible task. My mother fought me every step. She would call me and scream, "You're ruining my life. How can you give my grandbaby away?"

I knew I was capable of raising Adelia, with the help of my family and friends. I knew I could be a great parent. In my mind, I pictured the joy of bringing her home from the hospital. But that was not the plan my Lord had set before me. He allowed me to envision the even greater blessing for Adelia if I chose the *highest* good for her: a stable, loving home with a caring mother *and* father.

It was only because of God's peace gently calming my heart that I was able to withstand my mother's harassment. I was strengthened by God's grace every day. Now four years later, I still feel God's approval for the decision to allow Adelia to be adopted.

During the next few years, I again turned my back on God. When I became pregnant a year and a half ago due to a complete lack of judgment, I crawled back to my Lord. Humbly and once again afraid of the future, I begged for His help and for the comforting arms of my Savior. He was there for me. This time I did not sense that God was directing me toward adoption, so I began preparing myself for parenting.

During this pregnancy, I held down two jobs, lived with two of my friends, and attended church regularly. I found a supporting family at church, like the dear folks who had loved me at Fatherheart. These Christians welcomed me, loved me, and nurtured my soul and the soul in my womb with the Word and prayer. They celebrated with me at the birth of Russell.

During this time of rediscovery, I met Andrew, a quiet, thoughtful guy. I wasn't sure if he was part of God's plan for me. After much prayer I decided to give him a chance, and we dated. A year later, Andrew asked me to be his wife. Then he said, "I want to be Russell's father."

Thanking God, and with the peace that only He can give, I said, "Yes!"

We were married four months ago. Andrew has been a loving, protective, and kind husband and father.

◆   ◆   ◆

At times as I watch Russell Luke, I wonder if Adelia has the same mannerisms, or if she has the same laugh as he does, or if her look of love and admiration would be the same as his.

My adoption plan for Adelia was "semi-open," so her adoptive parents send me letters and pictures. I can follow her progress and am able to see how beautifully her family loves her. I know one day I will get to tell her how much I love her.

One day I will also see my son, Malachi. It will be a glorious day when all my children can meet and play in the yard of our Father's house.

◆   ◆   ◆

I know my decision to abort Malachi was wrong, wrong, wrong. But I thank God for giving me peace and for healing my guilt and depression.

I know it was the right decision to give my precious Adelia the gift of a loving adoptive family who could provide the nurture and support that I, as a high school student, could not give.

And I know it has been the right decision to parent Russell. I thank God that He sent my dear Andrew to be Russell's father.

As I look back I can see how God sent just the right people into my path just when I needed them. And I can now see that when I made wrong decisions it was because I turned away from Him. But God was always been there drawing me back to Him.

—*Noelle Aguirre*

Chapter Sixteen

God's Plan

If you are suffering because of an abortion...please know there is help and hope.

If you are considering an abortion...please know there is help and hope.

God offers...
- Inner peace, even in the middle of stormy circumstances,
- Inner joy, even in the middle of unhappy situations,
- Inner calm, even in the middle of chaos, and
- Guidance and direction, even when there doesn't seem to be a way.

You may feel like you're caught in a violent thunderstorm. In the midst of blinding streaks of lightning, jarring explosions of thunder, and pounding windblown rain, it is hard to imagine that the terrifying circumstances will pass. But always, after the darkness and chaos of the storm, come calm and the fresh smell of new life. God understands your desperate, stormy circumstances. He knows that no one chooses abortion lightly, and He wants to walk with you out of the darkness into His glorious light. It is only though Him that we can win the victory.

As you read the stories in this book, did you identify with the difficulties and pain? Did you notice how each story contributor eventually realized the importance of reaching out to God for help and forgiveness?

What should you do? Start by realizing that God loves you and wants you to be one of His children. *Because those who are led by the Spirit of God are sons of God. Now if we are children, then we are heirs—heirs of God and co-heirs with Christ. (Romans 8:14 and 17a)*

How do you become His child? We can find the answer in the Bible, God's Word.

> **First**, we have to realize we are sinners. *For all have sinned and fall short of the glory of God. (Romans 3:23)*

> **Second**, we have to be sorry for our sins and be willing, with God's help, to change. *Repent, then, and turn to God, so that your sins may be wiped out, that times of refreshing may come from the Lord. (Acts 3:19)*

> **Third**, we need to recognize that God provides for the forgiveness of our sins through His son, Jesus Christ. *For God so loved the world that he gave his one and only Son, that whoever believes in him shall not perish but have eternal life. (John 3:16) But God demonstrates his own love for us in this: While we were still sinners, Christ died for us. (Romans 5:8) In Him we have redemption through his blood, the forgiveness of sins, in accordance with the riches of God's grace that he lavished on us with all wisdom and understanding. (Ephesians 1:7)*

> **Fourth**, we need to believe that Jesus is Lord, the Son of God, and that He died and was raised from the grave. *That if you confess with your mouth, Jesus is Lord, and believe in your heart that God raised him from the dead, you will be saved. (Romans 10:9)*

So what must you do to become a child of God? The Bible verses you just read tell us you need to:

1. Realize you're a sinner

2. Be sorry for your sins and ask God to forgive you
3. Believe that Jesus is God's son, that He died on the cross to pay the penalty for your sins, and that He was raised from the grave
4. Be willing to surrender your life to Him and invite Him to be the Lord in your life

If you agree with these points and they describe what you are feeling in your heart, then what? Just talk to Jesus and tell Him:

> *I know that I'm a sinner. I'm sorry for my sins and I ask you to forgive me. I believe that you are God's son. I believe that you died on the cross to pay the penalty for my sins. I believe that you rose again. I surrender my life to you. I want you to be the Lord of my life. Please live in my heart and help me to be the person you want me to be. Thank you, Jesus.*

If you made the decision to invite Christ to be the Lord of your life, congratulations! This is the most important decision you will ever make. The Bible says you are now a child of God. *Everyone who believes that Jesus is the Christ is born of God. (1 John 5:1a)*

If sometime in the past, you had already invited Christ into your heart and life but have turned away from obeying Him, please know He is eager for you to return to Him. Ask Him to forgive you and choose to seek His ways—which are so much better than anything we can choose for ourselves.

◆ ◆ ◆

Welcome to God's family! He will bless you as you seek to honor Him and He promises victory to His children! *For everyone born of God overcomes the world. Who is it that overcomes the world? Only he who believes that Jesus is the Son of God. (1 John 5:4a, 5)*

This chorus from the song "Victory in Jesus" by E. M. Bartlett says it well:

"O Victory in Jesus, my savior forever.
He sought me and bo't me with His redeeming blood;
He loved me ere I knew Him, and all my love is due Him,
He plunged me to victory, beneath the cleansing flood."

That includes victory over the devastating aftermath of abortion. And victory over the pressures to choose abortion.

◆   ◆   ◆

You have made the first giant step by turning to God or returning to God. Others are eager to assist you on your journey to peace and joy. They have traveled the same road and have discovered the rainbow after the storm. They are available to listen and minister with compassion and love. See the list of helps in the Appendix that starts right after this chapter.

◆   ◆   ◆

God's Holy Spirit now lives in your heart and will guide and help you. *Because you are sons, God sent the Spirit of his Son into our hearts, the Spirit who calls out, "Abba, Father." So you are no longer a slave, but a son; and since you are a son, God has made you also an heir. (Galatians 4:6,7)*

Now that's really something to celebrate!

This is my prayer for you:

May the God of hope fill you with all joy and peace as you trust in him, so that you may overflow with hope by the power of the Holy Spirit. (Romans 15:13)

—Barbara Horak

Editor's note: If you prayed and invited Christ into your heart,
I would love to hear from you. Please contact me through
www.RealAbortionStories.com.

Appendix

Organizations, Programs and Support Groups, and Resources for Healing

---

Did you recognize your own situation as you read these stories? There are people who care and who want to help. There is hope, and there is healing!

What type of program or resource would be useful for you? To help you decide, read the article by Leslie Graves, which you can access at www.AfterAbortion.org/healing/index.htm.

Inclusion in the following list does not represent endorsement by the editor or publisher. Because websites change from time to time, if you are unable to access a site, try www.Google.com or www.AskJeeves.com or another search engine to locate.

Organizations

- **The Abortion Recovery International Network (A.R.I.N.)**
  www.abortionrecoverydirectory.com. Click on "Site Map," then click on your state to find nearby resources.
  A.R.I.N. maintains a database of abortion recovery support programs and services.
  Telephone: 1-949-679-9276
  Email: help@AbortionRecoveryDirectory.org

- **Care Net**
  Supports a network of more than nine hundred pregnancy centers and sponsors **Option Line**. Call 1-800-395-HELP (395-4357) twenty-four hours a day, seven days a week to talk, get your questions answered, and connect with nearby pregnancy centers.

- **The Elliott Institute**
  www.AfterAbortion.org
  Click on "Healing," then click on "Help After Abortion Page."
  Provides information, resources, and links to other resources.

- **Focus on the Family**
  www.family.org
  For a list of articles and resources, click on "Pregnancy Centers,"
  then "Hot Topics," then "Post-Abortion."
  Telephone: 1-800-A-Family (232-6459)

- **Lumina**
  www.PostAbortionHelp.org
  A referral network to put you in contact with those who can help.
  Telephone: 877-LUMINA1 (586-4621)
  Email: lumina@PostAbortionHelp.org

- **The National Office of Post-Abortion Reconciliation and Healing**
  www.NOPARH.org
  Click on "aftermath" to see steps to begin the journey to healing.
  Telephone: 1-800-5WE-CARE (593-2273) for assistance.

- **NOEL**
  www.NoelForLife.org
  From "After Abortion" menu, click on "Resources."

- **Pregnancy Care Ministries**
  A ministry of the North American Mission Board of the Southern
  Baptist Convention.
  Call 1-800-962-0851 for a referral to the nearest Pregnancy Care
  Center.

- **Priests for Life**
  www.PriestsForLife.org
  Click on "After Abortion" for links to information, resources, and
  programs.

- **Project Grace**
  www.ProjectGrace.com
  If you are computer savvy, you'll love this website.

- **Silent No More Awareness Campaign**
  www.SilentNoMoreAwareness.org
  Click on "Need immediate help after your abortion?" to see a list of resources. A Project of *NOEL* and *Priests for Life*.

- **Word of Hope**
  www.LutheransForLife.org
  Click on "After An Abortion."
  Telephone: 1-888-217-8679

Programs and Support Groups

- **Abortion Recovery Counseling, Education & Outreach**
  www.AbortionRecoveryCounseling.com
  Click on "Programs Offered" for group workshops, individual mentoring, and ongoing support.
  Telephone: 1-949-679-9276

- **Grief Net**
  www.GriefNet.org
  Click on "Adult Support Groups," then scroll down to "Loss of Child," and click on "grief choice."
  Offers email support groups.

- **H.E.A.R.T.** (Healing the Effects of Abortion-Related Trauma)
  H.E.A.R.T. is a biblically based program designed for use within pregnancy centers, counseling agencies, or churches. It is published by Heartbeat International. To find a program that offers healing after abortion, contact the Option Line at 1-800-395-HELP (395-4357) for the program nearest you.

- **Healing Hearts Ministries**
  www.healinghearts.org
  This organization also provides one-to-one email and support group counseling. In the left column click on the title. Allows you to sign up for an online Bible study.
  For women: A Bible study entitled *Binding Up the Brokenhearted*.
  For men: A Bible study entitled *Wounded Warrior*.
  Telephone: 1-360-897-2711

- **National Helpline for Abortion Recovery**
Free, confidential assistance by those who have personal experience with abortion and the healing process. Available twenty-four hours a day seven days a week. Coordinated by Concepts of Truth, Inc.
Telephone: 1-866-482-LIFE (482-5433)

- **Option Line**
Available twenty-four hours a day seven days a week to listen, to answer questions, and to connect you with nearby pregnancy centers.
Telephone: 1-800-395-HELP (395-4357)

- **Project Rachel**
www.HopeAfterAbortion.com
A healing ministry of the Catholic Church providing one-on-one care and counseling. Click on "Where To Find Help," then click on map to locate the Project Rachel nearest to you.

- **Rachel's Vineyard**
www.RachelsVineyard.org
A ministry of Priests for Life offering Christian help in a group setting, usually at weekend retreats.
Telephone: 1-877-HOPE 4 ME (467-3463)

- **SaveOne**
www.SaveOne.org
Click on "Post Abortion," at the top of the page. Offers a free twelve-week course.
Telephone: 1-866-329-3571

Resources

- ***A Solitary Sorrow: Finding Healing & Wholeness After Abortion***
This book by Teri Reisser and Paul Reisser, M.D., is available at www.GriefNet.org/library or www.family.org/resources/itempg.

- ***Aborted Women Silent No More***
This book by David C. Reardon is available at www.afterabortion.org. Click on "Resources."

- *Forbidden Grief: The Unspoken Pain of Abortion*
  This book by Dr. Theresa Burke explains how to help loved ones, or yourself—and what steps will help in healing. It is available at www.AfterAbortion.org, www.RachelsVineyard.org, or www.family.org/resources/itempg.

- *Forgiven and Set Free*
  This post-abortion Bible study by Linda Cochrane is available at www.parable.com. At "Search," type in "Forgiven and Set Free."

- *Forgiven: Finding Peace in the Aftermath of Abortion*
  This book by Christina Ryan Claypool is available at www.ChristinaRyanClaypool.com. Click on "How to Order."

- *Her Choice to Heal: Finding Spiritual and Emotional Peace After Abortion*
  This book by Sydna Massé and Joan Phillips is available at www.RamahInternational.org. Click on "Ramah Resources."

- *Men and Abortion: A Path to Healing*
  This book by Dr. C. T. Coyle is available at www.family.org/resources/itempg.cfm.

- *The Post-Abortion Kit: Resources for Those Suffering From the Aftermath of Abortion*
  Includes two books, a booklet, an information sheet, and a cassette. Available from Focus on the Family at www.family.org/resources/itempg.cfm.

Give the Gift of
Real Abortion Stories
to Your Friends and Colleagues

CHECK YOUR LEADING BOOKSTORE OR ORDER HERE

❑ **YES**, I want _____ copies of *Real Abortion Stories* at $7.95 each, plus $2.95 shipping per book (Texas residents please add 90¢ sales tax per book). Canadian orders must be accompanied by a postal money order in U.S. funds. Allow 15 days for delivery.

My check or money order for $_____ is enclosed.

Name _____

Organization _____

Address _____

City/State/Zip _____

Phone _____

Email _____

Please make your check payable and return to:
Strive For the Best Publishing
8900 Mettler Drive
El Paso, TX 79925-4047

To order with a credit card, please order online at
www.RealAbortionStories.com